The Wildwood King

Philip Kane

GW00646575

The Wildwood King

©1997 Philip Kane

ISBN 1 898307 68 7

Cover design by Paul Mason
Cover illustration by Marc Potts

Published by:

Capall Bann Publishing
Freshfields
Chieveley
Berks
RG20 8TF

Contents

By the same author:

Prayerbeads and Ravenbones

City's Little Heart

The Industry of Letters (as joint editor)

Desert Flowers

Introduction

In the course of writing, this has become a workbook of sorts. I have found myself including a series of exercises within the text, having learned that meaningful exploration of the Land must become experiential and not merely literary. But at the core of the book are the old stories. These seedpods of the traditional kenning will reveal little as long as they are left to lie dormant upon the page. Telling and retelling the stories yourselves, lifting them from the book and into life, is as essential to the development of a deepening personal relationship with the Land as is working through the various practical exercises.

I make no claims to be an expert or an authority on anything. From my own point of view this book, as with any other book, is part of an ongoing process of evolving ideas and, hopefully, insights. There are some implications in these pages that I am already following further; and probably many more that I have yet to be made aware of.

Full responsibility for any mistakes or idiosyncrasies remains my own, yet I would like to acknowledge those who have had some part to play in the gestation of this book.

I am grateful to my teachers, Inner and Outer. To the members of our coven, especially Li Sula and Tryfyth, who patiently experimented with the exercises. To all the fellow-storytellers whose conversation has helped in cultivating my own thoughts on the art, particularly Bill Lewis and Rob Parkinson. To Cat Summers, for publishing earlier versions of some of the exercises, in Pagan Voice. Jon and Julia Day at Capall Bann deserve mention for their forbearance in waiting for the manuscript. Profound thanks are due, also, to Diane for her unstinting love and support, and to Natalie for turning the music down while I write.

The Place of Storytelling

Writing a book centred on traditional stories is in many ways a contradictory process. The stories themselves have emerged from an oral tradition that reaches back to the first light of prehistory and perhaps even further, to a time of dreams and pre-conscious awareness. There is a sense in which writing them down falsifies them. The folktale takes on life in the telling; it gains power from the exchange between the storyteller and the audience. Whether overtly or not, all traditional stories induce a form of participation - it is the very air that sustains them as living, breathing organisms.

Write a story down and the danger is that it will become ossified, another dusty exhibit in the anthropological museum. That is not my purpose. The folktales that follow, or rather my versions of them, should be seen as creatures of the present moment. They are by no means to be regarded as somehow definitive. When I work with them myself, beyond the artificial boundaries set by this book, they change and are renewed with each telling; subtly altered by my own moods, by the impetus of a particular audience, perhaps even by some hidden internal process of their own. So regard each story as a sentient being in its own right, treat it accordingly with respect for its integrity, and it may unfold a deeper meaning than we are familiar with finding in a mere fiction.

It is difficult to define the essence of a concept as fluid and as variegated as that of "story". But I will take a risk and offer labels for some of the ingredients that seem to have been thrown into the cauldron of folktale.

Story comes into being as a means of organising perception of the world. The fact that the outcome of this organisation is so often ethereal, nebulous and elusive, may indicate the primal nature of the human mind. The story seeks to explain where science may not, it engages with "the reality behind reality". Why was the world made? Why is humanity separated from the other animals? Why do we die? And so on. For many societies, too, the process of story has organised perception on more mundane levels; telling which plants are edible, and which poisonous, giving each landmark and tree a history and a personality. Stories work to create a sense of place.

This sense is not a scientific or intellectual construction. Stories inhabit a realm of "metaphorical truth" which has an existence somewhere beyond the frontiers of rationality. This is not intended to imply that traditional stories are irrational; rather, they are non-rational. Neither is it to say that they can be reduced to the status of a "mere" metaphor. Story operates simultaneously on a multiplicity of levels of understanding and is its own reality.

Where do stories begin? Presumably once upon a time...A friend of mine has told me the following story[1]:

****

Among the Inu people of North America there is an old tale of the "stiff-legged bear". It is such an old story that nobody, now, can tell from where it came, or how it began. But anthropologists, being anthropologists, were

4

not satisfied with leaving such matters alone. They began to hunt the stiff-legged bear, in their own way, from place to place and from culture to culture. Gradually they came across other versions of the same story, among many peoples and in widely separated locations. At last, in one particular community, the anthropologists tracked down the most ancient stiff-legged bear of all. They were astounded to learn that the tale was, in fact, a memory of a woolly mammoth.

****

The origins of stories are so antique as to be effectively untraceable. The process of continual change ensures that memory and perception shift like soft sands to cover the trackways of oral tradition. The woolly mammoth shapeshifts to become a stiff-legged bear; Goddesses are transformed into a Queen of the Planets and a Sleeping Beauty. Those of us who tell stories can experience this flow from one aspect to another at first hand, sometimes sending even newly made tales out into the world only for them to come back to us wearing different clothes. The stories are not particularly diluted in this way. They are simply learning a revitalised relevance, at times even going into clever disguise to survive repression.

The stories travel far, too. In her little book *About the Sleeping Beauty*[2], P.L. Travers retells five variants of the same essential story; German, French, Italian, Irish and Bengali. Found versions of the Cinderella motif now number in the hundreds. The ubiquitous Nasrudin has made his way all around the Eastern Mediterranean, has ventured as far as Sicily and France, and made a home in contemporary Britain. Within its deceptively simple shell a folktale can encapsulate a kernel of wisdom and knowledge that will emerge when it is needed, in many places, at many times.

The storyteller stands at the heart of a delicate web of meanings, resonances and cultural integrities. Weaving the strands together is a more difficult art than is immediately apparent from a first look at folktales, being a form of intuitive craft. Hence the storytellers have commonly been regarded as being touched by magic, along with poets and blacksmiths.

Yet paradoxically (and story will often play with paradox) everyone is, to some extent, a storyteller by nature. The structure of story organises not only perception but our communication of our perceptions. Tell somebody about your journey to work - you are telling a story. Recount a joke you heard - you are telling a story. This does not mean that all stories are equal in their density of meanings or in their mythic qualities, any more than a plate of silver will weigh the same as a plate of paper. All stories, though, are strung upon a thread of relationship stretched across time and around the globe.

There is an ancient Chinese idea much cited by some modern storytellers. According to this, the Ladder to the Moon leads up from the humbleness of Earth to the glory of Heaven; at its foot the simple anecdote, at its head the great mythologies. Other substructures of story...hero-tale and wonder-tale, riddle and personal history, cautionary tale and local legend...take up the intervening rungs, each new rung higher and of greater significance than the last.

This particular image carries implications with which I am unhappy. It suggests a cosmology in which the Earth is relegated to a status of permanent unworthiness; a perverse notion which this entire book cries out against. Moreover, it encourages the concept of a fixed hierarchy whereby value judgements may be imposed upon stories according to their static place within it.

It is a form of metaphor which may have suited the ruling elite of feudal Chinese society. However, it seems to me that some other symbolism would do greater justice to the muscular current of human thought, passion and belief that courses through traditional stories. In frivolous moments, an alternative and modernised version of the Ladder to the Moon has come to mind - the image of an escalator! The energy running through stories rises from the base of fragments and anecdotes to the mighty heights inhabited by the great myths; and then, empowered, flows back again to the bottom.

The fact is that storytelling in all its many forms is a living art. Living not only in the sense of a continued vibrancy and relevance. No story, however powerful and meaningful, can be made to breath without the necessary oxygen of an audience. There is a familiar misconception that stories, and folktales in particular, are only for children. Yet in traditional societies, in which stories and storytelling remain central to the continuity of communal perceptions, and the storyteller is a key guardian of heritage and culture, the stories are shared by mixed audiences of adults and children.

In our society the prejudice against folktales begins early. Some comments from a group of fifteen-year-olds with whom I recently worked, while generally positive, tended to criticise traditional material as being "kid-like" and "aimed at a younger age group than myself because they were a bit far-fetched". At the same time, the continuing popularity of written fantasy and macabre fictions is testament to the eternal need for magic, albeit a magic that is all too often trivialised or brutalised.

In terms of cultural value, the story has always been appreciated as more than a straightforward entertainment. The following tale has appeared in many guises[3].

****

There was once a man who went by the name of Rory O'Donoghue. Now, in the summer Rory worked casually on the farms, but in winter found he had to make his living in some other way. This is what he did. You see, Rory's wife was a wonder for knitting stockings. They were ideal for keeping the legs warm over a cold winter, so they were very popular.

Rory would travel from village to village and from town to town, going wherever there was a market or even a street corner from which to sell the woollen stockings. And of course, he had to walk everywhere, carrying over his shoulder a big bag holding a little food for the journey and as many pairs of stockings as he could stuff in it.

Well, once Rory was on his travels, walking to some town or other with his stockings, and it was a particularly long journey from home. So long, in fact, that come nightfall he was still on the open road through the country.

Rory looked up at the first stars in a clear, cold winter sky and he said to himself, *"It looks as though I'll have to be spending an uncomfortable night by the roadside, with only this bag of stockings for my pillow"*. He had eaten the few morsels of food he had been carrying, too, so that his stomach was beginning to complain loudly and his knees were starting to feel weak.

Rory was just searching about for the best place to stop and settle for sleep, when across the fields he saw a solitary light flickering, the light from a cottage window, no less. Hardly believing his good fortune, Rory hefted his bag for a final tired effort, and made his way towards it.

There it was, sure enough, a small cottage standing alone right by the road. Rory O'Donoghue rapped on the door with his knuckles, and almost at once the door was opened from within. Light and warmth flooded out into the night, and there framed in the doorway was a stooped old man. Rory opened his mouth to speak and ask for shelter, but before the first word could come out the old man said:

"Come in, Rory O'Donoghue, and be welcome".

Strange as it was that the old man already knew his name, Rory needed no further bidding.

"Put your burden aside, sit yourself down, and take the weight from off your feet", said the old man, gesturing towards two plush armchairs that waited by a blazing fire. Rory put his bag of stockings down by the door, then one of the armchairs slid over to him, nudged at the backs of his legs until he sat down in it, and carried him back to the fireside. A pair of slippers walked up and settled themselves upon his aching feet.

The old man sat across from him in the other armchair. *"Would you happen to be hungry now, Rory O'Donoghue?"* he asked.

"That I am", Rory said honestly, although in truth his stomach answered loudly enough for him.

The old man clapped his hands together. A large bucket went out the door, filled itself with water from the well, then came back in and hung itself by a hook over the fire. While the water was coming to the boil, the potatoes peeled and scrubbed themselves. Then they, and a haunch of meat that had been waiting, jumped together into the boiling water.

As Rory watched, his eyes growing ever bigger and wider with amazement, a white cloth spread itself on the table, the knives and forks and plates set themselves out. When they were cooked through, the meat and the potatoes hopped from the bucket onto the table. The meat carved itself while the potatoes served themselves out.

At last, the two armchairs took Rory and the old man to sit at supper. And it was the finest meal that Rory O'Donoghue had ever tasted.

When the meal was done, Rory found himself back by the fire again.

"Well, Rory, I'll tell you how I spend each night", said the old man, *"I spend one third of the night eating, and one third of the night singing songs and telling stories, and the last third of the night I spend in sleeping"*.

He looked at Rory sharply. *"Sing for me now, Rory O'Donoghue"*.

Rory was bewildered. *"That I cannot do for you"*, he said, *"for I cannot sing a note to save my own life"*.

"No matter", said the old man, *"but tell me a story instead, Rory O'Donoghue"*.

Now Rory was abashed. *"I'm sorry, but I cannot do that for you either"*, he said, *"for I do not know any stories to tell you"*.

The old man stood up abruptly. *"Well then, if you can neither sing a song nor tell a story, it's out onto the road you must go"*.

With that, he grabbed hold of Rory by the collar of his coat and the waistband of his trousers, and Rory had just enough time to pick up his bag of stockings before he was flung out of the cottage door, back into the cold night air.

There was nothing for it but to start looking again for whatever shelter there might be in the open countryside. Rory began to walk along the road, if only to try to keep a little warmer. He had not gone far when he saw a man sitting at a campfire by the roadside, roasting a piece of meat on a spit.

"May I share your fire for the night?" asked Rory.

"Of course you may", answered the stranger, *"but would you mind turning this meat for me while I relieve myself.*

So Rory took hold of the spit and the stranger disappeared into the darkness. As Rory sat there, turning the spit, his attention started to wander and the spit turned more and more slowly.

"Don't you go burning my whiskers, now", the piece of meat shouted at him angrily.

Rory leapt up in alarm and he flung the meat on the spit as far away from him as he could. To his utter dismay it came back after him. Rory took his bag, turned and ran down the road as fast as his legs could carry him. But at every step the meat on the spit was with him, beating him on his back and shoulders until he was covered with cuts and bruises.

At last, Rory saw a cottage door. He hammered upon it with his fists, the door swung wide, and he fell inside. He was safe at last. When Rory looked up, he saw the stooped old man.

"What has happened to you, Rory O'Donoghue?" the old man asked.

Rory poured out the whole story; the stranger by the road, how the meat on the spit had shouted at him, then chased and beaten him.

"Now if you'd had that story in the first place, Rory, I would never have had to throw you out of my cottage", said the old man, *"There is a warm bed here for you now".*

Rory, then, had comfort for the night. Yet when he awoke the next morning, he was no longer snug in a bed. Of neither the cottage nor the old man was there any sign whatever. Rory was lying in the open by the roadside, his head pillowed upon his bag of stockings.

From that day to this, Rory O'Donoghue has always had a story to tell to anyone who will listen.

****

This story, as with all stories, may be interpreted simultaneously upon many levels of understanding. It can be seen as a cautionary tale reinforcing cultural values of hospitality and reciprocal generosity; or as a good-humoured warning about dealing with the strange and often mischievous inhabitants of the Otherworld. At the same time, the core of the tale is the cultural centrality of story (and songs can be seen as another story sub-structure), and particularly the role of story in confirming relationships.

In the Twentieth Century we have learned to perceive stories, at least traditional stories, as a wayward memory of an earlier, simpler age which our apparently more sophisticated society has matured away from. The folktales of an oral culture have been sidelined by literacy and literature, relegated to the status of a minor amusement for very young children, only occasionally accepted in the insipid, trivialised format of a Disney animation. Yet the old stories have a tenacious way of reappearing in modern guise, in the themes and plots of fantasy fiction and serious literature, in TV soap operas and in the theatre.

We tend to assume that we have a power over story because we are the tellers. Without human beings to repeat and embroider, story cannot exist, let alone flourish. Yet also, perhaps, it is the story which draws the outlines of our lives and threads, enigmatically, into our futures.

It is the structure of story which defines us, acting as a symbolic template that shapes our consciousness of love and justice, courage and wisdom, rights and wrongs. So the structure of story is necessary to us because it forms and directs our own sense of autobiography and ethics within certain cultural boundaries.

Story plays a critical role in our social interactions, as well as in our private selves. In love, for example, we usually expect to "*live happily ever after*". We are aware that, as in the story of Rory O'Donoghue, if we receive hospitality then we are expected to give something in return. The traditional stories still create a map to guide us through life as part of a community. The relationships that we form with others are moulded by the mythic influence of stories, and subsequently confirmed by them.

To be sure, there are more than enough voices arguing that the oral tradition, notwithstanding its historical importance, has become thoroughly outmoded; to retain their significance folktales must be reframed using modern media; to try to sustain an oral tradition of storytelling is just silly sentimentality. Yet in recent times a substantial minority of adults have once more been making a space in their lives for that same "childish" and "primitive" pastime of telling and listening to stories.

There is something here of a reaction against the threatening passivity and fragmentation of contemporary life. Storytelling is of necessity a communal activity, a sharing of experience and symbolism that taps deep into an old sense of community and continuity of tradition. In the face of a world in which control is exerted by fewer and fewer people, where the mass of us are urged to consume ever more blindly the trinkets turned out by modern capitalism, where individual lives seem increasingly beset by uncertainty and mischance, familiar communities disrupted and atomised, the metaphorical truth of stories not only keeps meaning intact, but becomes still more meaningful.

****

A certain African government once decided to install television sets in all the villages. They believed that it would prove to be a good way of both educating and controlling the rural population.

It was noticed by an anthropologist living in one village that at first the locals deserted their storytellers and began to sit around the new televisions. But after a short time the situation was reversed. People abandoned their televisions and returned once more to listening to the storytellers,

The anthropologist was puzzled. Surely, he said to the villagers, the television knew more stories than their old storytellers. "*Yes*", agreed the villagers, "*That's true. The television does know more stories. But the storytellers know us"*.[5]

****

There is also, in the allure of the storytelling art, an element of active involvement of the hearers. The act of storytelling is a ritual act in which the audience is a participant in remaking the pattern of the story. On one level, this inclusion of the hearers in the process may be reduced to a simple matter of audience response. On another, the specific way in which the teller moulds the retold story is intimately formed by her or his relationship with the audience. In other words, the height of the storyteller's art is to stimulate a form of 'altered state of consciousness' in which the unfolding imagery of the story takes on the dimensional depth of reality, and in which the dynamic rapport between teller and hearer energises those images with the significance of inspired insight[6].

It is important to emphasise the nature of storytelling as ritual in this context. The apparently extraneous actions of the storyteller in creating a location for the art somehow separated out from the everyday, in developing a persona of "storyteller as other", and in the use of linguistic devices such as opening invocations and chants, are all in actuality intrinsic elements of trans-forming performance into magic[7].

This book is founded upon two assumptions, both of which underlie subsequent chapters and at times break to the surface, where they are explored further.

The first of these is that the traditional story retains its ongoing vitality as a living contact with the Unconscious. Generations of psychologists and other thinkers have grappled with the problem of both comprehending and explaining this aspect of consciousness, and have usually found that their efforts have proved both flawed and controversial. Yet folktales, so often the literature of the illiterate poor, remain close to that formless, shifting sea of unconscious impulses, desires and longings that precedes and underpins the conscious processes of thought. There is no absolute separation, here, of rational intellect from non-rational sensation.

In folktale the Unconscious is given shape and the power of action. Kings, both clever and stupid, wise Queens, bold and handsome Princes, brave and beautiful Princesses, terrible monsters - all these have their existence within our own beings, on both the individual and the collective levels[8]. The many animals, too, that populate the stories are a part of ourselves; and this aspect may relate closely to the prevalence of animal totemism within so many traditional spiritualities.

The second assumption is that the human spirit and the physical environment of landscape and local distinctiveness are knit closely together. So closely, in fact, that seen holistically the interweaving of spirit and environment is such that they are inseparable, two elements of the integrated consciousness.

"We by no means rule over nature like a conqueror over a foreign people, like something standing outside nature...we, with flesh, blood and brain, belong to nature, and exist in its midst", wrote Friedrich Engels[9].

Engels saw the relationship in the context of a narrowly materialist sensibility. A broader materialism can argue that we "belong to nature" in our minds as much as in our bodies. This concept of an integrated consciousness I have chosen to term "the Land".

16

The emphasis implied, by this particular label, of the environment and the collective over the individual, is a deliberate emphasis. The stories through which we will proceed to pick our path will lead us to some landmarks of the relationship; and we ourselves will experiment, on our way, with the process of deepening and fulfilling a sense of intimate connection to the Land.

The Mother of the Forest

There was once an old woman who grew so weak and feeble that she could no longer work. Her family were poor, and often the poor must learn to be hard hearted in order to live. So they turned the old woman out of their house to fend for herself as best she could.

She wandered away, into the forest, where she plucked berries and dug up roots with her bare hands in order to eat.

The wild animals saw her walking here and there searching for food. For several days they watched her, and all the time she became less and less strong. Pity welled up in their hearts, and they met to discuss what they should do.

"*If we do not act soon*", they agreed, "*the old woman will surely die*".

"*I won't allow her to die*", bellowed the buffalo, "*I will adopt her as my own mother and care for her myself*".

The lion and the leopard spoke together. "*We will adopt her as our mother, too, and make sure that she always has food*".

The elephant spoke with dignity. *"Then I will also adopt her as my mother"*, he said, *"and she will not want for anything"*.

Just then, a great black cloud shut out the sun and glowered over the assembled animals. Rain began to fall, thunder rolled like many drums beating together, and forked lightning flashed down. Even as the animals ducked for shelter, the lightning spoke.

"I will adopt this old woman as a mother", she hissed and crackled, *"I will care for her and protect her from now on, as a daughter should"*.

They were all as good as their word. The elephant built a hut for his mother, thatched it, and kept it in good repair. The buffalo prepared a vegetable garden for her, digging, planting and tending. The lion and leopard hunted on their mother's behalf and brought meat to her each day. The old woman was contented, safe and well-fed.

Then one dawn she was awoken by a terrible sound. At first she thought that the sky itself must be cracking open like a nut. Yet when she peered outside she saw something much worse.

Over the forest there came flying an enormous bird. Its beating wings seemed to stretch from horizon to far horizon, compared to their noise the clapping of thunder would sound no more than the falling of a leaf. Its opened beak could have swallowed an entire village whole.

The earth itself shook as if with fear as the monstrous bird landed in front of the old woman's hut.

"Old woman, old woman, come out, come out", called the bird, *"I am the Master of All, I conquer all. So mighty am I*

that I make lions and hippos into finger rings. Come out, old woman, and tend your garden for me now, or I will kill you".

The old woman really had no choice. The bird stood over her while she worked in the garden all the long day, and only flew away as dusk approached. The woman was at last able to stop work and went into her hut to rest, weak and trembling.

That evening the buffalo came to visit her.

"Mother, you look so ill and you are shivering. What has happened?" he asked.

When the old woman told him about the great bird and its threat to kill her, the buffalo flew into a red rage. In temper he butted the trees with his horns and he pawed at the ground with his hooves.

"How dare this bully threaten my mother and force her to work", he shouted. "Don't worry, mother, tonight I will wait in your hut and when he returns I'll teach him a lesson".

So the buffalo slept that night in the old woman's hut and with dawn they awaited the bird together. Sure enough, the bird came flying to the hut, the sky darkening as its wings shut out the new-risen sun. It landed and began strutting up and down, the earth trembling beneath its feet.

"Old woman, old woman, come out, come out", called the bird, "I am the Master of All, I conquer all. So mighty am I that I make lions and hippos into finger rings. Come out, old woman, and tend your garden for me now, or I will kill you".

Hearing these words, the buffalo grabbed hold of the blanket from the old woman's bed and covered himself with it, quaking with fright.

"*Go out there and do as he wants*", pleaded the buffalo, "*Quickly, mother, before he kills us both*".

So the old woman went out into her garden and the bird stood over her, glowering, while she worked all day until she was weak and weary. When the bird at last flew away with the last light the buffalo crept, ashamed, into the forest.

Later that same night the lion and the leopard came to visit their mother, bringing meat from the day's hunting.

"*Mother, poor mother*", they said when they saw her, "*Your hands are swollen and you are shaking with fatigue. What has happened to you?*"

When the old woman told them about the great bird, how he had threatened her and forced her to work in her garden, they were furious. They roared with anger, their tails lashed at the air, they leapt at the trees with their claws unsheathed.

"*How dare he threaten our mother*", they both snarled, "*Tonight we will both wait here with her and when he comes again we will teach him a lesson*".

So that night the lion and the leopard slept in the old woman's hut, and as dawn came they waited with her for the bird.

It did come, of course, its wings casting the whole forest into shadow. It landed before the hut.

"*Old woman, old woman, come out, come out*", it thundered, "*I am the Master of All, I conquer all. So mighty am I that I make lions and hippos into finger rings. Come out, old woman, and tend your garden for me now, or I will kill you*".

When they heard this, the lion and the leopard both bravely hid themselves under the old woman's bed.

"*Do as he tells you, mother, please, before he kills us all*", they begged.

So the old woman went outside and the bird strutted about, watching her, while she worked all day. By the time the bird flew away at dusk she could barely stumble back to her own bed.

The lion and the leopard slunk away, ashamed and silent, into the forest.

That same night the elephant came calling and found the old woman still lying in her bed, too exhausted to even bathe herself.

"*How is it that you are so weak and helpless, mother?*" he asked her as he gently washed and fed her.

She told him about the great bird and he was enraged. With his trunk he tore whole trees from the ground and flung them aside. His tusks tore at the bushes and his angry trumpeting sent the smaller animals of the forest scattering in panic.

"*Who does this bully think he is?*" the elephant shouted, "*I will wait here tonight and when he comes in the morning I'll teach him a lesson*".

That night the elephant slept close by the hut, and with the first light of morning he hid himself carefully behind it.

The great bird came flying with the dawn, and when it landed the whole forest shook.

"*Old woman, old woman, come out, come out*", the great bird called, "*I am the Master of All, I conquer all. So mighty am I that I make lions and hippos into finger rings. Come out, old woman, and tend your garden for me now, or I will kill you*".

When he heard this, the elephant began to tremble. Carefully he thrust his trunk through the wall of the hut.

"*Go quickly, mother*", he whispered, "*Do as he says or he will kill us both*".

The old woman had no choice but to go out and do as the bird ordered. It kept her working in the garden all day, while the elephant stayed in hiding. As dusk fell the bird rose into the air on its huge wings and flew out of sight. Only then did the elephant show himself, going silently back into the forest with his head bowed down in shame. The old woman, meanwhile, could hardly crawl back to her hut, almost broken by exhaustion and pain as she was.

She had reached the threshold when a deeper darkness veiled the face of the night sky. At first the old woman cringed with terror, thinking that the bird had returned already; but then she felt the first droplets of rain and she looked up. Storm clouds rolled across the forest, and covered the moon and stars like a blanket.

Eerie lights flickered deep within the clouds.

"I have come to visit you, mother", the lightning said, *"But why do I find you weary to the point of death? Are you sick?"*

When the old woman told her all that had transpired, the lightning lit up in a fury. She flashed and streaked across the sky, she split trees into two and burned them to charcoal.

"Don't worry, mother", the lightning hissed, *"I will wait with you tonight and when that bird comes at dawn I will teach him a lesson".*

When morning came so did the great bird. Yet so many and black were the clouds in the sky that there was little light, so that this time the bird cast no shadow upon the forest as he approached. He landed before the old woman's hut and began to parade about imperiously.

"Old woman, old woman, come out, come out", it commanded, *"I am the Master of All, I conquer all. So mighty am I that I make lions and hippos into finger rings. Come out, old woman, and tend your garden for me now, or I will kill you".*

The storm clouds boiled angrily. The lightning blazed down and struck the great bird through its thick feathers, blasting it into a hundred pieces that were hurled in all directions across the forest. Again and again the lightning struck, until her terrible anger had burned itself out.

Afterwards, the old woman lived contentedly, cared for by her many children, until she died.

As for the great bird...the humans who lived in the forest found the burned meat that was all that remained of it, and they held a feast. I know, because I was there myself, and it was a fine feast too.

****

What is the Land? A landscape painted on the awareness or the memory, a stirring within the Unconscious, or a tradition borne from generation to generation like a seed upon the wind? It is all of these things and it is more than all of them.

The Land is an underlying pattern within the human psyche, just as with the sexual response. The concept of the Land is a part of the unconscious framework upon which we hang our responses to the world. The Land is an element of each and every one of us; yet, simultaneously, each and every human individual is an element of the Land.

Humanity and the Land are, ideally, a fused whole. Affect one, and thereby affect the other. Heal humanity, and heal the Land. Heal the Land, and heal humanity.

It is vital to reject unequivocally the dross of racial and nationalist ideologies, that some have tried to falsely associate with this notion of the Land in the past. The nature of the Land cannot be reduced to suit such superficial and reactionary fantasies.

The Land exists as a state of consciousness, of which physical landscape is but one expression. Of course the landscape can have an effect upon us, upon our individual and group consciousness. However, the landscape itself is created by the state of consciousness described as the Land, of which our own human consciousness is also an aspect. Physical characteristics are an outer manifestation, not an inner reality.

Through the patterns of traditional stories we can see that the fundamental nature of the Land is cross-cultural. That is, the essence of the Land remains broadly similar in whatever region, in spite of local cultural divergences. There is a common thread of perception, ritual and cultural practice at the root of traditions of the Land.

The Mother of the Forest fulfils an ancient dream of integration with the Land. It is not, originally, her choice to seek that dream. Her new life begins with pain and loss, with her abrupt expulsion from the normalities of human society. As with a succession of prophets, she goes out into the wilderness, to become a 'Wild Woman of the Woods'[1].

And the initiative in her actual process of integration is not her own, it is taken by the wild beasts of the forest. Our normal response to such animals is one of trepidation, at least, if not of outright fear. Our distance from wild nature is reflected in this, and in our consequent attempts to sometimes impose ourselves on nature, sometimes reduce it to a plaything. The latter reaction is arguably the source of the image of wild beast-as-pussycat promoted by some zookeepers, and of crude Disneyesque anthropomorphism. Such approaches to the wild, in my own view, only devalue the power of wildness and of animal nature.

This is not the whole story of the relationship, however. The wild creatures continue to live a parallel life on the Inner and the archetypal levels of human consciousness, as companions, as guides, as totems and as dream images.

Much has been written about individual, personal animal totems elsewhere, and I do not plan in this book to add to what has become something of an occult genre. I will only go as far as commenting that much of the existing literature on the subject seems to have the most meagre of connections with native British traditions[2]. This is especially true where an attempt has been made to "Europeanise" native American teachings.

Yet the truth remains that some variant of animal totemism has been historically relevant to each culture. The animal totem, the personal contact with and expression of the wild, is usually associated with the individual. What is important to us here is that animal guardians may also be linked to particular locations.

Sometimes this form of contact, this guardianship of a specific feature of the Land, has survived through the medium of folklore and legend. Examples might be the black dogs of Winsford Hill in Somerset and of Birdlip Hill in Gloucestershire; and water-horses, linked with numerous rivers throughout Scotland, Wales and England[3].

Occasionally, too, it is possible that an association has remained on an apparently superficial level, in place names. A swift look at my own local maps shows Hogshaw Wood, Hart Hill, Crowshole and Oxley. I would not wish to imply that *every* place name that might suggest some sort of animal is an indication of the "totem" of that place. There are often plain and ordinary reasons for such names. But even then it can sometimes be argued that there is a deeper, unconscious root to the material reasoning, and it is worth considering the name as a starting point when searching for the guardian of place.

More frequently the Outer memory of ancient associations has been lost. The sacred landscape of our ancestors has become increasingly mundane beneath the accretions of empirical thought. Recovering that landscape is an act of spiritual archaeology, yet the treasures that may be unearthed have a continuing value and potency rather than being museum pieces.

Before moving into the first practical exercise in this book, it is important to touch upon the actual role of these "totems of place". To begin with, it must be remembered that these animal-forms are but one expression of an energy, an energy which is often moulded by our own subjective experience. Thus, to some extent the otherwise shapeless force inherent in a location may "shape change". It is quite possible for it to appear in the image of, say, a human character as well as that of an animal. The energy itself remains the same, whatever its appearance at any given moment. Aside from simply "being" as the spirit or soul of place, this same force will act as a literal Guardian capable of acting to protect its own environment. This is reflected in the story of The Mother of the Forest by the actions of the buffalo, the lion and leopard, and the elephant, or at least by their intentions.

****

Exercise 1: Sacred Landscape

The sacred landscape still exists under the layers of thought which have reduced it to being "just" earth, rocks, or whatever. This first exercise begins the process of digging for the original contours of the Land.

Start to look for associations between sites within the local landscape and particular animals. Maps can help here - place names are a good area to begin with - as can local myths and legends. But far more important is to actually know the Land intimately.

Set out to travel through the landscape. Especially, walk the paths through woods or valleys or over hills. Many such paths are very ancient and still haunted by the spirit of old wisdoms. Listen carefully, as you walk, for the associations that arise from your Unconscious mind. These may be many or few; either way, do not try to force the pace, just allow images to "float" in your mind's eye. When you think you have an idea of an animal totem, be sure that you make a record of it, and of the place with which it seems to be linked.

Does anything appear in the form of dreams? The exercise will not be particularly successful unless you are able to immerse yourself in this quest for a time. This is the first step in personal attunement to the Land.

As you progress with the exercise, you should begin to see patterns emerging. By physically walking upon the body of the Land, you are enabled to feel its pulse, its life-force, through the medium of its physical features. Now begin to ask yourself; how do the animal guardians relate to the environments with which they are connected? Patient meditation will allow you to trace the bonds between the place and its spirit, and to comprehend the individual characteristics of each guardian.

Here, in outline at least, is a brief example. A few miles from my home there is a large wood, much of it planted by an aristocratic owner within the past two hundred years, but some of it still ancient woodland. The area is large enough that when this exercise was first worked there, the workers assumed that it must have more than one animal totem; the atmosphere changes markedly between different parts of the wood.

Eventually, however, following repeated contact with the environment, it was concluded that although a number of such Beings populated the wood, one Guardian stood over them all. The animal image which occurred again and again in connection to this particular woodland was that of a stag.

Further meditation on the image of the stag indicated an extreme wariness of human contact. At first there seemed to be no explanation for such caution, until we subsequently discovered how badly the wood was suffering from human activity - caused by joyriders, fly tippers and other problems from adjoining urban areas. All of this was to colour our subsequent workings with the wood and with the Guardian concerned.

****

The animals of the forest take the old woman as their mother. There is rather more contained in the implications of this than a simple act of charity. The relationship here is one of kinship, not of straightforward dependence. The unspoken suggestion underlying this aspect of the story is that the old woman, as Mother of the Forest, takes on a role with responsibility towards the other creatures. Integration with the Land entails an exchange of energies. We cannot take from the Land without giving something in return.

Materially this may, on one level, take the form of environmental activism. But the story of the Mother of the Forest suggests that what is demanded is a more specific and direct involvement with our environment. If the features of our sacred landscape each have their own distinctive characters and needs, as reflected in the characters of their guardian "totems", then each demands and deserves individual regard and nurturance.

Such an approach may involve, at the simpler end of the spectrum, taking on the task of clearing litter from a site when we visit. At a deeper level we might wish to work ritually with a particular place, thereby intensifying our connection through the intuitive, instinctive layers of consciousness.

Yet the story of the Mother of the Forest takes us even further than this. When the old woman seems to be safely settled in her new home, she finds herself confronted by a great and evil bird. We may see in this her meeting with her own Shadow self, her own dark accumulation of fears and personality distortions cast in a terrifying form. Her relationship with the animals of the forest is insufficient to save her from this Shadow. Eventually it is the more impersonal force of the lightning which comes to her aid, whereas the animals are themselves struck down by fear when the bird comes.

What does the lightning represent, within the terms of reference of this story? I would argue that, beyond the individualities of localities and guardians with all their unique characters, the Land as a whole has no overall consciousness, somewhat akin to the Collective Unconscious of humanity. The scope and power of this higher consciousness is a difficult concept for the individual human mind to comprehend, let alone to reach and make contact with. Neither is the road leading in that direction an easy one either to map out or to follow. Nevertheless that is what we will seek to do, on the way pointing out some of the pitfalls that await the unwary traveller.

The Lake of the Seven Swans

Once upon a time there was a wide lake, a lake known to all as the Lake of the Seven Swans. Only these birds, pale and otherworldly, lived there. Not another creature would go near to the place the deep waters were empty of other birds and of fish, the animals in the fields and in the woods shunned it as a drinking place even in the dry heat of summer. And filled as they were with fear, no man, woman or child would go down to the Lake of the Seven Swans.

The Seven Swans were dreaded by everyone. When the Swans took to the air, good folk hid within the shelter of their homes. Barring all the doors and shuttering all the windows, all night they would tremble in fear for their lives and their souls at the sound of great wings beating like the drums of demons, at the wierd cries overhead.

Then it so happened that a terrible time came to the place and the people. Famine came stalking over the land and there was no food to be had, certainly not for the poor and at last not even for the rich. There was no food to be bought, neither for love nor for money; there was not a scrap of food to beg or to steal. It was the fiercest of times and, as usual, the first to begin starving to death were the old ones and the children.

In that village, going hungry along with all the other people, there was a young huntsman. A bowman he was, a splendid shot, his eye always clear and his hand always true. There was not a living creature that could outrun him, when he chose to make it his quarry. This young man could no longer bear watching as the children starved. He grew daily more determined that he must do something to save them. Yet the fields and the woods had been hunted clear away until there was nothing left alive to hunt, and every stream had been fished empty. Nothing at all was left but the Seven Swans themselves.

So it was that the huntsman decided to take up his bow and his arrows and to go hunting after the Swans. In that time it was against the royal laws to hunt swans, which were said to belong to the King himself, but by the huntsman's reckoning these were not the King's swans. To his thinking these were the Seven Swans, and they were no man's property. The huntsman felt sure it was better that they should die in order that the children would live. Believing this, he went to the hunt.

Out onto the Lake of the Seven Swans he went, in a small boat. He hid himself deep among the tall grasses near the shallows, and waited patiently. When, at last, the Swans rose into the sky, the huntsman took aim, and he fired his arrow straight and deadly. Sure enough, it struck one of the Swans through the wing and the creature plummeted into the water.

As swiftly as he could, the huntsman rowed his boat over to draw her in, but as he reached to lift up the limp body of the Swan, the other six Swans came swooping down at him. They thrashed him with their wings, their beaks pulled and stabbed frantically at his clothes. The huntsman, in desperation, reached for his knife, his iron knife. As soon as he held it up, the Swans suddenly reeled away from him. They took flight, circling once before they flew away crying, and he was able to pull the wounded bird into the boat and to carry her back to the security of his cottage.

But once he was there, and the door shut behind him, a strange mood came over him. Instead of killing the creature straight away, for some reason the huntsman felt a kind of pity for it, and he bound up the wound. He wrapped a bandage tightly around the injured wing to stop the bleeding. As he looked up from binding the wing, he was astonished to see the Swan's feathers fading. For a moment his vision seemed to blur, and he found before him not a Swan but a young woman.

She was a woman who was more beautiful than any woman he had ever known before. From the moment he beheld this woman he felt a desire for her, a lust that surged up from within him like a great wave, and he was determined to have his way with her. He put his arms tightly around her and although she fought against him, he paid her struggles no heed. He pinned her closely in his embrace and there he took her, time and time again, their limbs entwining like root and branch of the trees in the forest. All the while that he used her, she cried and called with the haunting cry of a Swan, and she begged for mercy too, but the huntsman would show her none.

For seven long days and seven long nights he would only laugh at her cries, mock her despair. For seven long days and seven long nights her six sister Swans flew overhead, angrily beating with their great wings against the roof of the cottage. Still he laughed and scorned their fury. But after a while his laughter turned into fear, for what he had done was a crime against the Seven Swans. Nobody had ever done such a thing.

When the seven days and seven nights had passed by, the wound was healed. The huntsman thought that if he set the Swan-woman free, she and her sisters would feel gratitude and leave him in peace. But as he removed the bandage from the woman's arm, to his horror and his amazement he saw white feathers and down spring from the place where the wound had been. Even as he looked, the woman's neck stretched and grew sinuous, her whole body became covered with soft down, then with feathers. Before his wide eyes the woman was transformed back into the shape of a Swan.

She was a Swan that hissed, that raged, that beat her wings angrily. She went flying at the huntsman, she chased him out of his own door, out of the cottage and into the open.

There her sisters were waiting. They swooped down from the sky, and together the Seven Swans lifted the huntsman bodily from the earth, and they carried him far out over the lake. They held his head beneath the water, held it there although he struggled, until he was still, until he had drowned. And when the dead man floated face down on the lake, the Seven Swans took to flight. They circled in the air, seven times they circled over the water, and then they flew away beyond the mist and the rain, never to be seen again.

To this day that lake lies empty. No creature will go near the place. The deep waters are empty of birds and of fish, the animals in the fields and in the woods shun it as a drinking place even in the dry heat of summer. And filled as they are with fear, no man, woman or child will go down to it. For it is the Lake of the Seven Swans, and it lies there still.

****

The realms of the Unconscious can be a forbidding place, with their own dark guardians dwelling there. The depths of the mysterious Lake of the Seven Swans may be perceived as a symbol of the Unconscious in this respect. The presence of water in myth and symbol often plays such a symbolic role.

Swans, too, feature repeatedly in old tales. As do swan maidens, similar to the Seven Swans, for instance in the myths of Wayland the Smith and of Cuchulain. Modern psychoanalytic interpretations have, it seems, tended to categorise these majestic birds, as they appear in the human imagination, as indicators of higher thoughts and aspirations.

Certainly it is true that the swan, in many traditions, has earned a regal place; in Britain, all swans are regarded as the property of royalty. Yet swans, particularly in Celtic traditions, play a multiplicity of roles, primarily being linked with both love and death, and are closely associated with the Otherworlds of faery.

There can be no real doubt that the Seven Swans are such creatures of faery, shape-changers and guardians that they are. The lake itself serves to reflect a vital teaching; that states of consciousness may be manifested in physical form within the landscape. The physical location or feature resonates with the energies of an Inner state to the extent that the two become inextricably bound together.

Approaching the Lake of the Seven Swans, we are moving through an imagined aspect of the Land. No less powerful for that. The process of story weaves an Inner landscape, creating real, if often subtle, effects upon our physical reality and upon our perceptions.

Within this context, the Seven Swans represent something of our own personal Guardian, that shadow lurking on the threshold of the Unconscious, who we must pass in order to progress on our individual path to growth. This shadow may assume many forms. It can be a swan, it can be a terrible monster bristling with fangs and claws, or it can be a faceless sense of dread. It can also, however, take on a less threatening shape, turning from swan to swan maiden.

This aspect of the Guardian is that of the helper and guide, is revealed when we overcome our own fear. The young huntsman, in the story, is forced over and beyond that obstacle by the imperatives of privation. He must conquer his own foreboding or die, and know that those who depend upon him will die also. So he sets out to hunt and kill a swan, and must meet with the consequences of his subsequent actions.

The shadow has many places to lie in wait for our approach. Most critically, it may wait not only in the recesses of consciousness, but in the world of physical reality also. Fear of this Guardian easily becomes translated into fear of crossing the boundaries of the Land itself. As with most modern town-dwellers, who grow ever more fearful of wild places and of darkness. Various models of consciousness and growth touch upon this. For some traditions of the Craft, "where there is fear there is power"[1], while transpersonal psychology seeks to "turn blocks into stepping stones"[2].

For most of us, both the natural world and the Unconscious have become, almost in their entirety, forbidden places. Keep to the public footpath. Only explore the country of your own mind under the direction of the proper authorities. The Guardian, waiting in the shadows, has become a security guard and a psychiatrist.

The Seven Swans, however, appear as animal guardians of their lake, as the "totems of place' discussed in the previous chapter. The restrictive and more recent roles have been grafted onto the original characteristics of such guardians by the psychic disturbances within our own consciousness. Before we can relate effectively and properly with these guardians, we have to learn how to deal with our own Inner distress when confronted with the forbidden places.

Until then, we are always in danger of reacting in the same fashion as the huntsman, seeking to exploit that which he does not understand and so cannot work with. His own psychic disturbance is expressed in the attempted killing, and the rape that follows. His own fear is held in an iron grip, a forced servant to his will, rather than explored, remodelled and transcended. As the huntsman acts, so does humanity respond to those aspects of the Land which lie beyond the scope of our materialist understanding. Repeatedly wounding it and, if the cliche may be excused this once, raping it.

The exercise that follows is a visualisation of the type that is commonly called a "pathworking". Prepare yourself by sitting comfortably on a chair, preferably one with a hard back, and take a few minutes to relax both mentally and physically. Then close your eyes and begin to visualise the "story" of the Path to the Lake as it is described. It is best to have a friend read out the pathworking to you, or to record it on tape beforehand. Leave pauses in suitable places.

When you come to the end of the pathworking and return to full everyday awareness, it is a good idea to "ground" yourself again with a hot drink (not an alcoholic drink) and something light to eat[3].

Exercise 2: The Path to the Lake

Imagine that you are sitting in a chair. In front of you, just a few steps away, there is a door. It is wooden and arched, with a heavy looking black handle.

As you look at it, the doorway swings slowly open, to reveal a track beyond. On the other side of the door it is an autumn morning. A lingering mist coats the hedgerows on either side of the trackway with a thin grey wash. Standing up from your chair, you step out onto the track and walk a little way. You see that the hedgerow is made up from a mixture of small trees and shrubs, but is mainly of hawthorn, whose red berries appear faded in the mist. As you walk along you can detect a leafy smell, carried on the cool breeze.

Dewy strands of cobwebs cling to you, as they are stretched and broken from the bushes on either side. It seems that you are the first on the track today.

You can see that the track curves round to the right and is lost from view. You walk on and, as you turn the corner, you see that the path has become very overgrown.

Grass and cow parsley, heavily laden with dew, brush against your legs and arms, making them wet. The track leads you down a gentle slope, but shortly levels out. Here the hedgerows broaden out to form the boundaries of a wood.

At first you feel hesitant about entering the wood. From where you are standing, you can see that it is a shadowy tangle of trees and deep undergrowth. You cannot see far along the track because it disappears from view a few yards ahead, as it begins to wind among the trees. Even standing here, peering into the woods, your mouth begins to feel dry and you are aware of a creeping sense of foreboding.

Nevertheless, you summon up your courage and begin to walk forward once again. The path seems to twist and wind beneath the treading of your feet, leading you deeper and deeper among the trees, until your sense of direction is all but lost.

Suddenly you realise just how still the wood is. There is no breeze to rustle leaves or rattle branches. No birds sing among the trees around you. You cannot even hear the usual scurryings of small creatures hurrying through the undergrowth. You are surrounded by a heavy and, you think to yourself, watchful silence.

With this in mind, you are beginning to quicken your steps, when abruptly you find that the path has led you through and beyond the wood. Now, before you and lapping almost at your feet, you see a broad lake. The lake appears to be as still and quiet as the wood that you have just traversed. No birds fly in the air above the lake or swim upon its surface. You watch the waters closely for a while, but see no evidence of any fish living there.

You approach the edge of the lake and sit down upon the bank. The waters are still and curiously black, and when you gaze into them your reflection peers back at you as clearly as if from the glass of a mirror. For a while your attention is held by this reflection of yours. The water ripples, and your reflection is fractured...and when the water stills and clears once more, your image is no longer before you. Instead other images begin to shape themselves as you look, fascinated, into the depths of the black and silent lake.

For some time you remain seated there, simply gazing. You try to impress upon your memory as many of the passing images, whether fleeting or long-lasting, as you possibly can.

The lake surface ripples again, the visions cease, your reflection reappears on the water. At last, your awareness of your surroundings returns. Something in your mind tells you that it is time to leave the lake. You stir, and stand. Turning, you walk back along the path the way that you came. The wood is still as before, but this time as you pass through it you feel no tremor of fear.

Coming out of the wood, you climb the gentle slope, between the hedgerows bordering the path. The mist has cleared now and the Sun is climbing in the sky, touching the Earth with a soft autumnal warmth. You feel the brush of the Sun, too, and realise how chilled your body had been as you made the journey to the Lake.

Pushing through the overgrown stretches of the track, you follow the bend round to the left and find yourself on the last part of the pathway. Ahead of you, at the end of the path, you can see the doorway through which you first entered this strange world.

You walk forward between the hedgerows on either side of you, coming closer and closer to the door. Now it is directly in front of you. The door swings silently open at your approach and, beyond, you see your chair. You step through the door, which gently closes behind you, and sit down.

Gradually become aware of your own world around you once more, and return to full consciousness.

****

There is a relationship possible with the forbidden or forbidding places, alternative to that which the huntsman had with the Lake and with the Seven Swans.

The physical features of the Land, such as the woods and the waters, have their own forms of consciousness. Given the attitudes of the majority of humanity to the Land for centuries past, the long legacy of estrangement and heedless exploitation, it is hardly surprising that often the Land should seek to hold humanity at bay, by generating an aura of suspicion, fear, and outright hostility.

It is this which can touch upon our unconscious link with the Land, triggering our own fears and confronting us with our own forbidden places, our own dark guardians. By altering our own perception and approach to the Land and our relationship with it, we may move towards a new and, as yet, rare psychic wholeness.

The Lazy Man and the Water-spirit

There was a man named Mulele. He lived with his mother, and he was so lazy that he would hardly lift a finger without some complaint. All he ever did was lie around, dreaming and drinking beer, of which he was very fond. But this Mulele had a very high opinion of himself.

"Life is unfair", he was always saying, *"I was not meant to be a simple man. I should be a chief, with wealth and luxury"*.

"You are an idle good-for-nothing", said his mother, *"Always drinking and wishing your life away. A chief needs willpower and self- restraint, but you have neither"*.

Mulele never listened to her. He only called for her to make more beer.

One day, it happened that Mulele's mother had no food for the cooking pot, so she sent her lazy son out to hunt.

"Don't come back here empty handed", she shouted at him, and she waved a stick to make her point stronger.

Of course, Mulele was far too slothful to hunt anything actively. He just went out and set snares here and there in the forest. Then he sat under a tree for the rest of the day, daydreaming and sleeping by turns. Late in the afternoon he finally stirred himself and went to check the traps. Sure enough, he found a partridge caught in one of his snares.

Feeling immensely pleased with himself, Mulele slung the partridge over his shoulder and he set off for home. It so happened that on his way he had to go by the river. As he walked along the riverbank, the water-spirit who lived there saw him passing and called out.

"Mulele, throw the partridge in to me. If you do, you will have not only food, but everything else that you desire".

The temptation of having all that he wished for without any effort was too much for Mulele. He turned and flung the partridge out into the waters of the river, where it landed with a splash and then sank quickly, leaving behind only a few ripples on the surface.

When he reached home his mother was very angry. She shouted, she stamped her foot, she waved her stick. But Mulele took no notice of her. He could think only of the promise that the water-spirit had made to him.

The next day, his mother sent him out to hunt again. She scolded him, saying, "This time, do not be such a useless idler, bring home meat for the pot or I'll make you rue the day you were born".

Still, Mulele had no interest in looking for game. He set his snares and then spent the day under a tree, sometimes asleep, sometimes thinking of all his wildest desires. Eventually he rose and looked at his traps. He was happy to find that he had snared a guinea-fowl.

With the guinea-fowl over his shoulder, Mulele went walking homewards by the river. As he had hoped, the water-spirit saw him going by and called out.

"*Mulele, throw the guinea-fowl in to me. If you do, you will have not only food, but everything else that you desire*".

Mulele needed no second bidding. He took the guinea-fowl from his shoulder and hurled it far out into the water. It landed with a splash and sank at once, leaving behind only ripples.

Now, as Mulele watched, the river near the bank where he stood began to bubble and foam. A voice came from the depths of the water.

"*Mulele*", said the water-spirit, "*I have promised you your desires and I will keep my word. But you must promise me one thing in return. All I ask is that you show enough restraint to play the dance-drums with your hands as a chief should, and not with drum-sticks like a poor man*".

Mulele promised readily.

"*Then all that you desire shall be yours*", said the water-spirit.

Before Mulele's astonished eyes, a gaping mouth opened in the river, the waters around the mouth growing redder and redder until they looked like a pair of lips. The mouth called, "*Reach down into me, Mulele, and pull out all that you find*".

Cautiously at first, Mulele put his hand into the mouth and pulled out a gourd. He reached again and pulled out a second; then a third; and a fourth.

On it went, until there was a great heap of sealed gourds piled up on the riverbank.

The water-spirit told him to take them home and break them, one by one, on the rocks behind his mother's house. Then the mouth disappeared, and the river was still.

Mulele gathered up the gourds and carried them home in a state of great excitement. His mother scorned and taunted him for bringing back such useless rubbish instead of the meat that she had wanted for her cooking pot. But Mulele ignored her as usual, and taking the gourds to the rocks he began to break them open.

As soon as he broke the first gourd, out jumped a row of strong youths who hailed and greeted Mulele as their chief. When he broke the second gourd, out came a row of beautiful young women who greeted him as their husband. When he broke the third, he was presented with an enormous pile of the most gorgeous clothing, which he and his mother quickly put on instead of the shabby skins that they had been wearing. He broke the fourth gourd, and there was a stack of hunter's guns. From the fifth there came many kegs of gunpowder. From the sixth gourd there came countless beads in every colour. From the seventh gourd a pile of thick, warm blankets. So it went on, and to tell of all that came from the gourds would take too many days.

At last, Mulele indeed had all that he desired. He was a great chief, with wives, warriors, fertile gardens, flocks and herds, clothes, music, rich foods, and all the beer that he could drink. He lacked for nothing, and he and his mother both lived their days in great pomp, waited upon hand and foot by their many willing and faithful servants.

It had all come very easily, so easily that Mulele was full of arrogance and empty of wisdom. He was fond of parading his opulence and power before the neighbouring chieftains. Yet Mulele never was able to lose his taste for beer. In fact, he spent much of his time so drunk that he was unable to attend to important affairs of any kind, much less properly administer the new domains that he ruled. Before long, the people began to despise the foolishness and the extravagance of their beer-swilling chief.

One day Mulele called for a great dance and feast. For the occasion, as usual, there were many huge jars of beer and Mulele made the most of them, drinking continually from noon until midnight. All was well until, at last, Mulele was so carried away by the effects of the beer and the excitement of the dancing that he snatched the drumsticks away from one of the drummers and began to beat enthusiastically upon the drum himself. No sooner had he struck the first sounds than there was a great "BANG!"

Mulele was flung backwards onto the ground. His head swam, his mind reeled. For a time he just lay on the earth, unable to see anything clearly. When the world came back into focus, he was horrified. His beautiful, shining robes had disappeared and he wore nothing but a loin-cloth of monkey skin. The many lithe dancers had turned into grasses that waved in the breeze. The blankets were just so many fallen leaves. The guns had become twigs. The countless beads were nothing but dust. Not a trace was left of Mulele's great wealth, and he himself was once more thin, half-starved and dirty.

His mother came towards him. She, too, was clad only in skins once more. She struck at him with her stick, shrieking, "I told you so! I told you so! You do not have the willpower and the self-restraint to be a chief."

47

Mulele was terribly depressed by his sudden loss. For some days he stayed indoors, not even rising from his bed. Then he thought of returning to the water-spirit to try to restore his fortunes.

He set out at once to hunt in the forest. Try as he might, all he managed to catch were a grey wildcat and a brown wildcat. He went straight to the riverbank, and called out, "*Water-spirit, shall I throw these wildcats in to you?*"

"*You may if you wish, and you need not do so if you do not want to*", replied the water-spirit with indifference.

Mulele threw both the wildcats into the river, one after the other, and watched them sink.

The following day Mulele rose early from his bed and once again went into the forest to hunt. Again, he tried his hardest but was only able to catch a grey wildcat and a brown wildcat. He took them to the river, where he called out, "*Water-spirit, shall I throw these wildcats in to you?*"

"*You may if you wish, and you need not do so if you do not want to*", the water-spirit said disinterestedly.

"*May I take some more of the gourds from your mouth?*" asked Mulele.

"*You may if you wish, and you need not do so if you do not want to*", replied the water-spirit.

Mulele could hardly contain his eagerness. He flung the two wildcats far into the water and watched them sink. The river, near to the bank, began to foam and to ripple. As Mulele looked, he saw the red mouth open as before. Plunging his hand inside,

Mulele pulled out first one gourd, then another, and another, until there was a great high stack of them beside him on the riverbank.

He carried the gourds home as fast as his legs would carry him. Breathlessly, he took them over to the rocks behind his mother's house.

Mulele broke the first gourd. Out came a black snake, which darted at him angrily.

He took up the second gourd, thinking he might be luckier this time, and broke it. Out came a crocodile, which snapped at him.

Yet Mulele was determined, and he missed his life of luxury. He broke a third gourd upon the rocks. Out came a scorpion, raising its poisonous tail to threaten him.

When he broke the fourth gourd, a long centipede crawled out and ran at him. At last Mulele, thoroughly disheartened, gave up.

His mother was very angry, and she shouted, "*Mulele, I want no more gifts such as these near my home. You may gather up all the gourds and throw them back into the river, where they came from*".

In sadness, Mulele walked back to the riverbank and began to throw all his gourds into the water, one by one. As he did so, the red mouth opened in order to swallow them.

When they were all gone, the water-spirit called, "*Mulele, you have learned now how it is useless to give wealth and ease to one who has not worked for it. My advice to you is to work hard from this day on, and practice some self-control. That way you will earn a peace that is never won as the reward for idleness and folly".*

Mulele took the water-spirit's gift of advice. He returned to his traps and his garden. He even learned to hunt quite well. Although he never became a chief again, neither he nor his mother ever wanted for food or clothing.

****

In 'The Lake of the Seven Swans', the huntsman has no communication with the Land. The result is his aggression, a violent abuse of the Land and its powers, which enacts his own inability to integrate the darker parts of his unconscious.

Mulele does have a relationship with the Land, through the medium of the water-spirit, which includes prolonged communication. But Mulele still manages to abuse this relationship. The problem for Mulele is his own laziness; or, looking at the story from the perspective of this current discussion, his eagerness to take from the Land while giving back nothing of lasting worth.

It has to be said that the easy route is always the most tempting one. From Mulele's point of view, being granted the gifts that come from the water-spirit must have been rather similar to winning the National Lottery jackpot in our modern cultural terms. Already a weak character, when fabulous wealth drops into his open hands the weaknesses are exaggerated until he manages to destroy his own overblown lifestyle.

It has become a truism of our contemporary ecological awareness that humanity has exploited the environment to the point of exhaustion, returning absolutely nothing in exchange for the use of immense natural resources. A truism, in fact, to the extent that it has been drained of much of the power to awaken our emotional attachment to the Earth and her treasures. We know it to be true, but for most people the knowledge arouses such feelings of powerlessness and despair that it has become far easier to settle into detachment from the Land, and a frantic enjoyment of the fruits of exploitation, than to face the responsibilities of an intensified relationship.

An extension of this is the search for a quick and easy route to some vague notion of enlightenment. We know that there is something deeply and distressingly painful damaging our kinship with the Earth, with the animals, with the wildwood. Yet even as we seek to correct imbalances, to heal the hurt, we still for the most part approach this work as consumers who would rather buy a quick cure than expend the time and energy involved in real healing.

So we snap up the latest product, whatever it might be; a new book to explain it all, imitation culture snatched from native Americans, the latest New Age therapy, or a new crystal. But nothing really changes.

Like foolish Mulele, all our wealth is just sand in the wind because we do not accept that we have responsibilities; because we do not accept that relationship, by its very nature, demands something from us in the way of commitment.

****

Exercise 3: The Gifts of the Water-spirit

Imagine that, like Mulele, you have come to the river's edge and that the water-spirit has spoken, offering you whatever you desire.

You may take up to nine gifts from the water-spirit. Take a sheet of paper and write down what you would wish to receive as your gifts.

But the water-spirit, in return, requires some commitment from you. Think about this carefully; taking the water-spirit's point of view, what might be asked of you? Write it down, whatever it is, somewhere underneath the list of gifts you have received.

Reflect, for a while, on these. Weigh up the gifts, and ask yourself what they say about you. Is the commitment that the water-spirit has demanded of you an easy one to keep? Or will you find it difficult? What does this tell you about yourself?

Now write the story of the gifts you have received. How do they affect your life? How do both the gifts and your experience with the water-spirit change your interaction with the natural environment and with the people around you? How is your perception of yourself changed? Write this story assuming that you keep your promised commitment.

When you have finished, put your story aside for at least one day. Then read it over to yourself again. Reflect on the story for a while. Did you really have all that you desired? Did you actually desire the gifts that you asked for? Did you find meeting the commitment easy; or did it test you? Would you, now, list the same gifts and the same commitment, or would they be changed? What does all this say about you?

Write an alternative ending to your story, an ending in which you fail to keep your promise to the water-spirit. Express how it feels to lose the gifts. Once more, put this aside for at least a day.

When you look at the stories again, compare them with one another. What are the similarities? What are the differences? Can you learn anything from this?

Finally, imagine that many years have passed and you have grown very old, so that it is almost time for you to leave this world. You have always kept your promise to the water-spirit, the gifts are all still in your possession. But soon you will have no use for them, so you have decided to give them away.

Decide who you will leave each gift to. Write a letter to go with each gift. Explain how it has been of value to you. Tell the new recipient how you hope the gift will be of value to them in the future. Reflect upon this.

****

It is always easier to follow the line of least resistance even if, ultimately, it leads us nowhere at all. There are, however, other paths which may be harder but which, eventually, are more rewarding. Esoteric tradition suggests that it is possible to make use of resistance in a similar way to a sprinter employing a starting-block. The resistance may become a source of power, rather than being an obstacle to be overcome or which simply blocks progress altogether.

This implies that exploration of the forbidden and forbidding places, commitment and challenge may serve us in expanding and extending our sense of personal power and, in the terms of this book, our sense of integration with the Land. It is to a challenge that we must next turn our attention.

The Harp on the Water

Long ago, so long ago in fact that people had not even begun to count the years, there reigned a King who was perhaps the most wicked King who has ever lived. This King lived in wealth and splendour, and his nobles grew fat, while the common people toiled and suffered and went hungry.

To celebrate his own power and opulence the King decided to have built a great stone palace, in the most fertile valley within the realm. Its cost was great; many farmers were dispossessed, the taxes raised to pay for the work leeched the poor until they were left white with starvation. And so many labourers died in the building of the palace that folk said that it had been built upon their bones. The huge palace was completed, however, and for many years it stood as a symbol of cruelty and oppression.

It came to pass that late one night the King was walking through the ornate gardens of his palace, thinking on new torments and persecutions that he could inflict upon his subjects. As he strolled along a particular path, he heard a small voice that whispered in his ear.

"Vengeance will come, vengeance will come", said the voice.

The King started. He looked ahead, to the left, to the right. He looked back over his shoulder. There was not a living soul to be seen. Yet he heard the voice speak again in his ear.

"*Vengeance will come, vengeance will come*", it said.

Now the King grew angry. He shook his fist, defiantly, at the night sky.

"*Let your vengeance come. I have no fear of it. Why should I? The walls of my palace are thick and strong. My armies are powerful. Seek vengeance if you wish, and be damned!*"

In fact the King became, if anything, more wicked than ever before. The wealthy loved him for they grew, year after year, wealthier and fatter still; while everyone else became poorer and weaker.

Time passed, and the King had three sons. If anything they proved themselves to be even worse in nature than their father. For his part, he merely encouraged their depredations while they rode about the countryside, leaving a trail of murder, arson, pillage and fear in their wake.

Late one night the King went walking through the gardens of his great palace. He thought on how well his three sons were growing, how proud he was of them all. He considered new taxes and new crimes for his courts to deal with, although the walls of the prisons already groaned and bulged outwards with the press of prisoners. Then, as he walked, a small voice whispered softly in his ear.

"*Vengeance will come, vengeance will come*", it said.

The King stopped abruptly. He looked ahead, to the left, to the right. He looked back over his shoulder. He could not see one living soul in the garden with him. But still, he heard the voice again directly by his ear.

"Vengeance will come, vengeance will come", it whispered to him.

The King was beside himself with fury. He raised his clenched fist and shook it at the night sky and the whole wide world.

"Let your vengeance come", he bellowed, *"I have no fear of it. Why should I? I am mighty, with three fine sons. The walls of my palace stand thick and strong. My armies are powerful. Seek your vengeance if you dare, and be damned!"*

If the King changed his ways at all, then he changed them for the worse, and his three sons followed suit. The people of his realm suffered as never before.

And then it seemed as if their nightmare of hardship and poverty might never cease. For a few years later one of the King's sons had a son of his own, so that the wicked dynasty was assured. The King was so exultant at the birth of his first grandchild that he declared that he would hold a great banquet at his palace for the nobles, and for the wealthy landowners and merchants. He invited them all to join him at the feast, and they came gladly. He ordered, too, that the common people should celebrate enthusiastically, on pain of losing their heads if they did not.

In particular, the King sent a company of soldiers to find a certain white-haired old harper who lived high up in the hills. The harper was summoned to play at the banquet for the pleasure of the King and his guests. At first the harper refused to obey, for he hated the King and his sons as did all commoners. But when, at last, the soldiers threatened to murder his wife before his eyes if he was not compliant, he agreed to go with them. He took up his beloved harp and, closely guarded, he trudged down from the hills, into the valley where the stone palace loomed like a glowering tyrant.

That night a thousand candles lit the great hall of the palace. Guests in dress of silks and furs crowded around the tables, gorging themselves on exquisite dishes and supping rich wines. The old harper sat upon a dais at the end of the hall and played for them, although it seemed that nobody actually listened. For hours he played, until his fingers were sore, until his hands and arms ached with strain. Yet he was not once offered a morsel of food nor even a drop of water.

At last, the harper was told that he was permitted a brief rest. Trying to soothe his troubled mind as well as his aching limbs, he wandered out into the palace gardens and began to walk, taking some comfort from the soft light of the Moon and the stars.

And as he walked, he suddenly heard a small voice that called, "*Come, follow me. Come, follow me*".

The old harper looked all around ahead, to left, to right, behind. He could see nobody. Thinking that his wearied mind must be playing tricks, he walked on.

He heard the voice again, calling, "*Come, follow me. Come, follow me*".

The harper looked about himself again but there was not a man or a woman to be seen. There was only the glow of candlelight and a bright tinkling of voices from within the hall. And a small brown bird that hopped on the path ahead of him.

"*I don't suppose that you spoke to me, little bird*", the harper said with a smile.

But the bird did speak to him.

"*Come, follow me. Come, follow me*", it said.

Fascinated, the harper did begin to follow it. Truthfully, he could not do otherwise but walked through the palace gardens as if in trance and unable to resist the bird's will. Further and further from the hall they went, and even though the harper knew that his own life and that of his wife would be forfeited if he failed to return, he could not turn back.

All the time the brown bird hopped on the path just a little ahead of him, calling insistently.

"*Come, follow me. Come, follow me*".

Through a small gate they went, out and away from the palace, across the broad valley and up the far slope. At last, on the heights overlooking the valley and the King's palace, the old harper was overcome by his tiredness. He sat down to rest awhile, and as soon as he did so he fell soundly asleep.

He was awoken the following morning by the sound of a small stream gurgling nearby. He opened his eyes and he was struck into stillness by the sight before him. For of the wide fertile valley, there was no sign. Of the great stone palace, there remained not a trace. All that the harper could see, stretching as far as his sight could reach, was a great lake, the waters of which lapped at his feet. And the only thing that moved was his harp, as it came floating gently towards him across the surface of the lake.

This is a true story. The proof of it is that the lake is still there. It is Lake Bala, in North Wales, and if you do not believe the story you may go there and see for yourself.

****

This Welsh tale has long been a personal favourite of mine. A cruel dynasty, with all its courtiers and supporters, with all its symbols of pride and wealth, is drowned and destroyed by the titanic, unstoppable forces of nature. It is a story which is not merely pertinent to a Welsh nation and culture repressed over many centuries; but which acquires renewed relevance wherever tyranny holds sway.

Even in the fairly recent past we have witnessed the same unswerving, relentless tide of vengeance. Each time that an oppressive regime falls, it is as if the great lake has risen up and swallowed it whole. In this sense the lake symbolises the elemental force of the people in all their accumulated wrath and potential power. It is an old association, the seething plebeian and peasant masses with the faceless waters of the Unconscious, with the wild and untamed aspects of Nature. There are numerous references to such shapeless, and often brooding, strength.

Certainly it must have seemed shapeless and brooding to the educated and privileged minority through most of human history. Theirs is a keen awareness tinged with both awe and fear; although for some, by 1818, the attitude was changing but not the imagery. In his great poem *Prometheus Unbound*, Shelley appeals for action to free humanity from tyranny and to make change, to the "mighty darkness" of Demogorgon - the people-monster[1].

In this respect, '*The Harp on the Water*' may be perceived as a story of hope in the face of a desperate situation. Perhaps, at one time, it was indeed a masterly work of agitprop, designed to sustain the morale of a subjected and oppressed populace, which would be only the more effective by working on the psyche of its listeners at the symbolic, non-rational level.

So how does this fit into our understanding of the human relationship with the Land? Simply this. If the human mind is itself a part of the integrated consciousness of spirit and environment we call the Land, then the connection of the people in the mass with the waters of the lake begins to reveal some interesting indications of a properly balanced relationship.

It is clear that in their arrogant and thoughtless brutality, their privilege, pride and acquisitiveness, the wicked King, his family, and the hierarchy of their supporters have cut themselves loose from the responsibilities that should bind them closely to both Land and people. The consequences are dire. Corruption, greed, and self-serving at the expense of the public good are rife. A true relationship with the people, with nature, with the Land, is not just neglected but held in contempt[2].

The implied moral is that, for those with some place of authority, the bearing of responsibility is not only an ethical choice but is also a practical imperative. Such an imperative applies not just to Governments, but at all levels of human life and society. Even the individual has a degree of privilege with regard to the environment. This has far-reaching implications when our human society has such enormous capacity to shape the environment to suit our own needs, even to the extent of carving and remoulding entire landscapes.

But the symbolism of this story, as with most, operates upon more than one level. This is not just political allegory. The characters of story lead an alternative existence as forms of archetype and sub-personality (to borrow a term from psychosynthesis). In this sense, the figures of traditional tales such as Kings and Queens take on the special density of symbols, signifying meanings above and beyond mundane powers and legal statutes.

There is plenty of literature discussing archetypes, both in general terms and in specific instances; and picking over the functions of archetypal images wherever they are thought to appear, especially within the context of dreams. There is a tendency to reductionism in some parts of this field, lessening the depth of our perception of such symbols. When the true nature of any symbol is to shift specific meanings like the tumble of colours in a kaleidoscope, it is a great deal easier to make a diagnosis if we can pin them to an absolute, fixed point in consciousness. In such terms of reference, we can swiftly interpret the King as a father figure, an impression of paternal authority strutting about, arrogant and domineering, on the stage of a collective neurosis. It is then quite easy to unravel the entire story as if it is a knot of Oedipal impulses.

Too easy, in fact. I would contend that there are major flaws in that particular approach to understanding traditional stories. Not least among my reasons is the fact that the kind of family structure existing at the time when such stories originated was fundamentally different to the bourgeois family that Freud, his contemporaries, and those who came after had in mind when they developed their theories.

We have to look to earlier, and less mechanistic, conceptions of symbolism. Here an awareness of the underlying philosophy of the Tarot - an ancient system of symbolism which actually predates the appearance of the familiar cards - may help. Broadly and very generally speaking, in the world of the Tarot the Kings represent way that we *think* and the Queens represent the way that we *feel*.

This is important, opening the story of 'The Harp on the Water' to our renewed understanding. There are two key points to be made.

The first of these is that we have, in this story, a dynasty made up entirely of Kings. Except by implication, the births of sons and of the grandson, the Queen and other royal women are absent from the proceedings. It is relatively uncommon, in folk tales, for any King to be long without a Queen, and vice versa. The balance of male and female polarities is usually maintained. So it seems unlikely that the missing Queen is a victim of sexist attitudes. However, her invisibility does emphasise the role of the King; and the story becomes clearly a story of intellect without the balancing force of emotion.

The second point arises from this. Without the presence of a strong emotional force, the intellect is corrupted, obsessed with domination and displays of grandeur. The vital bond with the Land is broken. And eventually, vengeance will come. The unbalanced intellect is drowned by the primal forces of the Land.

We may understand from this that the real weaving of the consciousness into the tapestry of the Land is a matter of emotional bonds, patterns of feeling and intuition, not of merely reconstructing our thinking. Also, the lesson to be drawn from the story, the ethic that is its kernel, is not just a lesson for the individual. As a society, we have degraded our emotional connection to our environment in favour of a hard, pure rationalism. We are still, on the whole, wearing the false crown wrought by the positivists - that we will one day count every particle in the Universe[3]. Nature, and by extension the Land, is regarded as subservient to our intellectual might.

Outer and Inner states and relationships have a tendency to reflect one another. If our Inner condition is imbalanced and corrupted, so are our perceptible responses to the world about us. If our material relationship to our environment is one of master to servant, this feeds back into our Inner selves, stunting the capacity to feel and to sense. Those who are at war with nature are at war with themselves.

This is a fundamentally unstable state of affairs. The Land itself will eventually seek to correct the imbalance. The intellect is at last drowned by the Unconscious that it has failed to accept and integrate. This is what the story of 'The Harp on the Water' has to tell us.

****

Exercise 4: Meeting the King Within

In this exercise, the intention is to meet and converse with the "King Within".

Begin by using your powers of visualisation. Imagine a proud and powerful King. What does he look like? How is he dressed? Gradually build up a mental picture of him and of his surroundings. Where is he? Perhaps he is seated upon a throne. Creating this image of the King will probably take a few attempts to complete; be aware that both his appearance and his surroundings may alter from time to time.

Remember that this King is a part of your own self, a symbol of your own intellect. What feelings and thoughts are evoked by the image?

Now "breathe life" into your image of the King. The picture that you have created within your imagination takes on increasing depth and realism. When you feel ready, be conscious of stepping into the image. Seek to begin a dialogue with the King. What are his strengths? His weaknesses? What is there that blocks his relationship with his realm and subjects? With his own Queen, perhaps? Does he have a message to give to you?

There will probably be questions unique to yourself, and questions that will arise in the course of any dialogue. And this exercise may be repeated as often as you wish, or need.

If you would like to develop the exercise further, try the same technique but using the images of the four Kings, and later on the Emperor, that are to be found in a Tarot deck instead of your own image. Each King may be considered as symbolising an aspect of the Inner self.

The exercise, as it stands, only highlights the strengths, weaknesses and blocks that may stem from the intellect. How you work with these is, of necessity, a personal matter. Think on this deeply.

****

The Discontented Grass Plant

Once there was a grass plant that grew by the estuary of a great river. He was just one stalk of grass among many millions, and therein lay the source of much trouble. For this was a very discontented grass plant. As the wind bent him this way and that, he dreamed of a better life, in which he would not be lost and nameless amidst his numberless sisters and brothers.

It so happened that late each Autumn, just as Winter was beginning to reach out long cold fingers to grip the Land, the women would come out from the nearby village in order to gather great piles of the grass. It was a kind of grass that grew tall and slender, good for weaving into baskets, or for braiding into thick mats and the soles of boots. The women would cut the grass close to the ground, and carry bundles of it home on their backs. Year after year they harvested the grass, but not once did they come near to the discontented grass plant.

The grass plant became more and more unhappy with his lot. He was always looking about, wondering what it would be like to become whatever he saw, wishing that he could change. One day he spotted a herb growing nearby. The herb was small and unremarkable. Yet the grass plant gazed at it longingly, saying to himself, "*How I wish I could be a herb*".

The wish had barely been finished before it was fulfilled. The plant no longer had simple long blades, but delicate lobed leaves instead. He had a branching stem, and even tiny flowers. For a while he felt contented and passed the days in peace and happiness.

Summer ripened. One day the women came back to the river. They carried knives and baskets. They searched around for herbs, using the knives to dig up whatever they found. Sometimes they would eat a tasty root, but most of the gathered herbs were put into the baskets ready to be carried home to the village, as medicines or for the cooking pot.

All day the herb that had been the grass plant cringed with fear and tried not to be noticed. The women went home as evening fell, leaving him still securely in the earth. But the fear lingered, the herb thinking that he might well be dug up another time. He was no longer content.

Once more he began to look about and wish that his lot could be otherwise. He spotted a clump of plants which had tubers at their roots. He began, again, to dream and to wish. He said to himself, longingly, "*I wish I could be one of those plants*".

He had hardly made the wish when it was granted. Now the plant had changed again, and had a tuber at his roots. For a while he was at peace.

One evening, as he stood there by the river, he saw a mouse scampering through the grass nearby. It stopped by a similar plant and began to dig, throwing soil in every direction. Then it pulled up the tubers from the plant's roots. It held the tubers one at a time in its tiny fore-paws, hunching over them and eating them quickly.

When it had finished, the mouse ran on, still looking for food.

It had not touched the plant that had once been a grass plant. Yet he was shocked by what he had just seen, and frightened. He said to himself, "*I am no longer safe like this. I wish that I could be a mouse*".

Instantly, the plant found that he had indeed become a mouse. He had grown fur, four legs and a long tail. Delighted, he began to run about through the grass, enjoying his new freedom to move. Soon, he felt hungry. So he dug into the earth as he had seen the other mouse doing, pulled up tubers, and holding them in his forepaws he began to nibble at them.

He went further and further from his old home by the river, every now and then stopping to eat more tubers, or standing up tall on his hind legs to look about. There was so much that was new and fascinating to see. For some days, the mouse that had once been only a grass plant was contented.

One night, the mouse stretched up inquisitively and saw something strange which made him quickly duck back down again. Not far away, a white spectre was gliding silently through the air, and it was coming closer. As the mouse watched, he saw that the spectre kept interrupting its eerie flight, diving to the ground briefly before rising up once more.

As this apparition came nearer, the mouse realised that it was not a ghost but a big white owl flying towards him. The owl spotted the mouse, too, and plunged down at him with sharp talons reaching out for the soft furry body. The mouse lunged away in terror, running for his life. He was lucky. Even as the claws of the owl were about to close on him, he came across a small hole and he darted inside.

The owl, thwarted of this particular meal, flew on soundlessly. Meanwhile the mouse, panting with fright inside his hiding place, was no longer so contented with his lot. His heart beat hard against his ribs. He said to himself, *"This world is not a safe place for a mouse. I wish that I could be an owl"*.

By simply wishing, his form was immediately changed. His fur became white feathers. Now he was an owl, with great noiseless wings that swept the night winds. He lifted gracefully into the air and turned towards the north.

He travelled for a long time, stopping to sleep during the day, now and then pausing to hunt and eat a mouse. Yet he was unused to flight and eventually his wings grew weary. When he was close to falling out of the air with tiredness he found he had reached the seashore. To rest, he settled himself upon a piece of driftwood that had been left standing upright, stuck in the sand of the beach.

As he sat there, he watched two young men go walking by. In his heart the old, familiar feeling of discontent began to swell up again. He said to himself, *"I no longer want to be merely an owl. I wish that I could be a man, such as those two youths"*. With a flap of his wings, he dropped to stand upon the ground. Instantly, the power of the wish turned him into a naked man.

Soon the night came swimming across the sea. The man who had been an owl sat down on the sand of the beach, with his back rested against the piece of driftwood, and he slept there until the morning returned.

This place was in the far north, where the nights are long and very cold. When the early light woke the man, he was stiff and lame as a consequence of sitting and sleeping in the chill air of the night. He searched about until he found some grass, and with this he wove himself a cloak that would help to keep out the cold from his body.

Not long after, he saw some reindeer grazing nearby. He felt hungry, and the desire rose in him to kill and eat one of these reindeer. Dropping to his hands and knees, the man crept close to the herd. Suddenly leaping at the nearest animal he seized hold of it, and with a single easy twist of his hands he broke its neck.

Slinging the carcass over his shoulder he walked back to his sleeping place. Then he found that his fingers could not pierce its skin, so that he could not prepare it for eating.

The man thought about this for a long time. He found a stone with sharp edges, and he used it to cut away and remove the hide from the reindeer. But he still had no fire over which to cook the meat. Looking around, he saw two white stones lying upon the beach. When he struck them together he was able to make sparks. Gathering together dry grass he managed to start a fire, then roasted some of the reindeer meat and ate it.

The night that followed was a very cold one again. In the morning the man caught, killed and ate another reindeer and the next morning, yet another. Each time he broke the animal's neck with a single movement of his hands, bore it over his shoulder to his camp on the shore, and skinned it with the sharp stone. Soon he was able to clothe himself from head to foot in reindeer hides. The nights were growing colder and colder. Bringing a great deal of driftwood to his camp, he built himself a simple but comfortable hut.

One day the man was walking over the hills near the seashore when he noticed a strange black animal eating blueberries from the bushes. The animal was a bear. The man caught hold of the bear by one of its hind legs. It turned to face him, showing its teeth and growling with anger. Grabbing it by its fur, the man raised the bear above his head. He flung it to the ground with such force that he killed it outright. He went home with the bear carried across his shoulders.

When the man skinned the bear he found fat, the oil from which he could use to light his hut. He hung the bearskin in the doorway to keep out the cold wind. He was able to live in this way for many days, but eventually he began to feel lonely.

At this time, thinking alone in his hut, he remembered the two young men he had seen walking along the seashore while he had still been an owl.

"*Other people must live nearby*", he thought, "*I will search for them*". So the next day he set out, going the way that the young men had passed.

He wandered along the coastline for some time, until at last he saw, drawn up on the beach, two splendid newly-made boats, with spears and fishing tackle in them. With great curiosity, the man examined these. Then he saw a path leading away to the top of a hill, so he followed it.

At the top of the hill there were two houses. Lying upon the ground were the bodies of two freshly killed whales, and the skulls of many other whales around them. Quietly the man crept towards the doorway of the nearest house. A skin hung over the entrance to keep out the cold winds. The man carefully lifted a corner of the skin and looked inside.

Opposite the doorway a young hunter sat cross-legged, working on some arrows. A bow lay close to his hand. The man who stood at the doorway felt fear, anxious that he might be shot, and let the skin drop back into place. Then he thought to himself, "If *I should enter and say, 'I have come, brother', he will not harm me*".

So grasping his courage, he raised the skin and entered the house quickly, saying, "*I have come, brother*". The young man leapt up and cried out with delight, "*Are you my brother? Welcome, come sit beside me*". The man who had once been merely a grass plant sat down eagerly.

The young hunter began to talk. "*I am glad that you have come*", he said, "*I always believed that I must have a brother, but no matter how hard I looked I could not find him. Tell me where you have lived. How did you grow to manhood?*"

For a long time they talked of their lives by the seashore, of living alone, and of hunting game for their food. The hunter said that in one of the houses on the hill he kept many rich furs, and in the other stored a wealth of food and seal oil.

At last night came and the two brothers fell asleep. They arose with the daybreak, and once they had eaten the hunter went out with his bow and arrows in search of game. He went by himself, leaving the other man behind to cook their meals.

They kept this arrangement for a long time, but eventually the man who had once been a discontented grass plant began to weary of staying home and preparing food.

"*Why can I not go out hunting with you?*" he asked his brother one day. The hunter refused his request, and started out alone again. But the other man came up softly behind him and grabbed hold of his foot. The hunter turned, growing angry.

"*Why have you followed me? You can kill nothing without a bow and arrows*", he said.

"*I can kill game with my hands alone*", the man said.

His brother, the hunter, was still angry. "*Go home and see to the cooking*", he said in a voice filled with scorn.

Instead of obeying, the man stalked a herd of reindeer and killed two of them with his bare hands, just as he had done while living alone. Then he stood, waving and shouting for his brother to come. The young hunter was both astounded and furious, because even with his bow and arrows he had not succeeded in killing any game at all.

The man who had once been a stalk of grass carried the two reindeer home upon his shoulders. The hunter followed with a darkness gathering in his mind and on his brow. Evil began to fill his heart. He knew much jealousy and anger. Fear, too, at the enormous strength his brother had displayed.

All evening he was sullen and withdrawn, hardly able to taste even the morsels of food he could bring himself to eat. Before long his behaviour and his suspicions had encouraged the same feelings in the mind of the other man.

They watched one another warily, each fearing treachery from his brother.

The next day was clear and bright, the sea calm. The men paddled the two boats far out, until they could no longer see the land. After a long time they turned back, both of them still discontented and unhappy.

"Now let us find out who can reach the shore first", jeered the hunter.

The two boats almost leapt from the water as they darted towards the land. First one seemed to lead, then the other. With a last great effort the two men raced their boats onto shore, and they sprang out onto the beach at the very same instant.

In rage they shouted at one another, *"You are no longer my brother. You go that way, I will go this way"*. They turned their backs on each other and separated forever, in great anger.

One man was changed into a wolverine. The other man was changed into a grey wolf. In these forms they may be seen wandering the countryside to this day. They are both always discontented and unhappy.

****

Change is the great constant. There is nothing in existence which is fixed, static, absolutely immutable.

Change is at the heart of the story of *'The Discontented Grass Plant'*. Over and over again the protagonist achieves change through his own will, changing himself rather than changing the world. Yet by doing so, his relationship to that world is also transformed through a series of successive shifts of perception. The hero, "who was once a grass plant", experiences his existence as both passive object and active subject, as both the hunted and the hunter.

Although the mythic realm of story is apparently distanced from the everyday world of our daily lives, the former reflects the latter. Contemporary society often seems to be obsessed with individual, personal change and growth. In the course of our own journeys we will see ourselves, our circumstances, our lives and the Land itself in myriad ways.

It is not only individual perspective that shifts and flows. So too does the Land. From the slow evolutions of geology to the cyclic nature of the seasons, from the gradual unfolding of human consciousness to the sudden impact of societies and cultures upon the natural environment, the whole range of elements that make up the "Gestalt"[1] of the Land are in continual flux, a state of perpetual motion.

Modern capitalism, especially, is the most revolutionary of all human societies that have so far existed. The changes emerge and develop with such rapidity that they overlap and overtake one another. The best rooted of traditions can be plucked from the Earth and swept away by tempestuous winds of innovation, which are not always negative. How to keep pace with revolution after revolution? The "shock of the new" still sends reverberations shuddering through the Unconscious. Increasingly, the quest for personal growth gathers the desperate momentum of a coping mechanism. Today, assertiveness training. Tomorrow, a change of wardrobe. The day after, meditation and creative visualisation. Then on to self-hypnosis, shamanism, therapy... Yet, somehow, it never seems to be enough of a change. Like the grass plant, we remain unsatisfied and at odds with the world around us.

A part of the special nature of story is that even when we, as listeners, are skilfully drawn into its magical web, we are still enabled to stand back upon a high vantage point and see far further than the characters. The grass plant, for example, is too closely involved to realise that his frantic transformations are, in the end, only surface changes. The Land itself walks a different path, which as a part of the Land he cannot escape. Perhaps, then, what is missing from the processes of personal change is the deeper awareness, the perspective that comes from standing upon a mountain.

****

Exercise 5: Lifelines

Here is an exercise which is designed to facilitate an overview both of your own life and that of the Land as a whole. You cannot know the movement and growth of the Land on a rational, intellectual level but you can develop some insight into the progression of totality. It is all a matter of altering personal perceptions.

The approach, essentially, is to envisage your life as a story. Begin with the present moment. Then start to trace the line of your life in reverse sequence. Which events stand out in your life? What are the strongest images that you have of particular events, times, people and places? Where are the points at which significant changes have taken place?

This will probably take some time to complete. Write everything down as you come to it. By the time you have reached back as far as you can go, you may well have filled up many pages. If, at any point in this exercise, you touch on something where you feel blocked from progressing, simply make a note that this block exists and then try to pick up the thread of memory again further on.

Eventually you will come to the starting point of your memories. When this happens, take a sheet of paper and on it draw a long, straight line. Now begin to mark off, on this line, the events, the people, places and so on which you see as being the key nodes of change in the course of your life.

Take some time to think about this. It is possible you will become aware of a pattern, or even patterns, contributing to the definition of your life path.

Now move on to the further stage of this exercise. Draw another line below the first one. Again, mark off the events, people, and so on, that you can recall from memory, but this time you are taking a wider view, exploring your memories of the wider community of major happenings that had implications for the world beyond the circle of your own life, of names and faces that may linger from the news.

Look for any patterns that may be emerging. How do such big events relate back to the line of your own life, if they relate at all?

There is a third and final lifeline. This last line attempts to trace the life of the environment within the range of your experience. Proceed as with the other two lifelines, but this time focus upon the changes in your environ- ment. You will probably have most success with fairly local changes, which you may have experienced more or less directly; but if a change further afield, or even maybe on the world scale, occurs to you in the course of this exercise do not neglect it.

Open yourself to an awareness of any patterns that might be perceptible running through and connecting these three lifelines.

****

Here we can begin to develop an overview of the Land, albeit a flawed one. Flawed because the genuine understanding of the Land's totality can only come about through non-rational processes, through a deepening personal involvement with the life of the Land itself.

So what, it may be asked, is the place of a comparatively rational exercise such as the 'Lifelines' exercise above? Miyamoto Musashi wrote that, "*Whenever we have become preoccupied with small details, we must suddenly change into a large spirit, interchanging large with small*"[2]. Although Musashi was writing about the nature of strategy, he saw no dichotomy between this and Nature itself[3], so that we are able to apply his words to our understanding of the ways in which we perceive and work with the Land.

The point is that we need to balance two views of the Land and its workings, its many shifts and changes. We must learn to fly from the mountain peaks down to the valley where the Land's deep currents flow like a river, then back again, as fluently as we are able. If we become too entrenched in the valley, too engaged with the non-rational, we may soon become near-sighted, turned inward and unable to follow or approach the wider forces impinging upon our consciousness. The non-rational eventually dissolves into the irrational. On the other hand, if we spend our time exclusively on the mountaintop we lack oxygen, become dizzy and detached, losing all sense of specific experience and of connection.

The 'Lifelines' exercise is also artificial to the extent that it construes time as having a purely linear, sequential structure. An important ingredient of the Pagan outlook is the perception of time as a spiralling state of consciousness[4]. It obviously follows from this that the 'Lifelines' exercise does not depict or demonstrate an absolute principle, but only forms a working model of reality which allows the individual consciousness to grapple with a totality that it could not otherwise comprehend.

We all tend to envision our lives as a series of labels put upon us by others, or which we take upon ourselves. Each change of label engenders further changes. When the herb becomes a mouse he no longer fears being taken from the Earth but he quickly learns to fear the owl. The problems of life do not wither away, they alter with our perceptions.

This can lead us to a form of conservatism, once this is realised, where change is fearsome and it seems better to maintain the status quo, however painful, than to face the growing pains of change. "Better the devil you know than the devil you don't know", claims an old saying.

The greatest problem with such conservatism is that efforts to cling on to the present, to freeze reality or turn it into stone, are always doomed to failure. Change must always come whether we will it or not. This is true of the Land as a whole, as well as being so with the lives of individuals and communities.

Whether any particular change is for better or for worse is often regarded as a matter of individual human judgement. But the totality of the Land, that blending of natural energies and human consciousness, is itself urging us in an evolutionary direction which has its own currents, which makes its own demands. From this understanding, some changes - especially certain human-made changes to our environment are quite definitely counter-productive. Those who are conscious of the Land and its needs have a responsibility to seek to correct the mistakes.

On the whole, however, we need to be aware enough to be discriminatory about changes, even those changes which have some ecological impact. Neither life nor the Land are static entities, and to be fully alive means learning to work with change rather than always against it.

To do this adequately requires an approach to deeper wisdom than that of the individual personality.

Who Owns the Land?

It happened that two farmers were deep in dispute over a particular piece of land. One day they met to discuss their differences.

Said the one, *"My father farmed this land, and my grandfather before him, and my great-grandfather before him. The land belongs to me"*.

Said the other, *"Go to the town and look there at the Public Records. I have it on paper that I own the land; signed and sealed by representatives of the government itself. The land belongs to me"*.

"You're a thief", said the first.

"You're a liar", said the second.

"Fool!"

"Imbecile!"

And so it went on, the argument growing louder and more fierce until the first blows had been struck and one of the farmers might have drawn his knife, had not passers-by stepped in and held back both men.

As hot tempers began to cool a little, a suggestion was made that there might be a way to settle the dispute without spilling blood. In the village where these two farmers lived, there also dwelled an old woman who was known for her skills with herb and spellcraft, and who was held in high regard by the villagers for her good sense and practical advice. In short, she was the kind of old woman who in another time and another place might have been condemned for her wisdom. To this woman a messenger was sent with an appeal to come and settle the argument between the two farmers for once and for all.

She came soon enough and she led both farmers - and by now, too, a crowd of curious onlookers - straight to the field that they both claimed.

Once there, without uttering a word, the old woman lay flat upon the ground with her head cocked to one side.

The two farmers waited expectantly for a few minutes, and it must be said in their favour that they at least tried to be patient, but their tempers had already slipped too far. Before long their rivalry was being given voice again.

"*You're nothing but a thief and a skulking bandit*", snarled the first farmer.

"*You're a liar descended from a family of liars*", growled the second farmer.

The old woman looked up at them. "*Be quiet, the both of you*", she hissed.

"*Why, what sort of trickster or fraud are you?*" demanded both angry farmers as one, "*We ask you to resolve a serious matter, and all you can do is lie upon the earth as if sleeping*".

The woman gave them a hard look and said, *"Be patient and be still. I am listening to what the land has to say"*.

Chastened, the men did as she told them. In time, the old woman stood up and brushed the loose earth from her long skirts. The farmers both looked at her with hopeful expressions.

"Well", they both asked, *"which of us does the land belong to?"*

The woman smiled and said to them, *"The land says that you belong to Her"*.

And isn't that the truth?

****

This is just one variation upon a story which recurs in many cultures. There are two other variants on the essential theme of the Land's ownership that are pertinent to this discussion. One of these features the ubiquitous Mulla Nasrudin[1]. The other appears in the thirteenth century *Prose Edda* of Snorri Sturluson[2].

Nasrudin, who is sometimes referred to as remarkably foolish, and at other times as impossibly clever, is substituted in the role of the Wise Woman in a story originating from Turkey. Given that the Nasrudin tales have penetrated as far as Russia, Sicily and France, often attributed to more regionally recognisable characters, it seems reasonable to assume that the basic form of this story has travelled in the Mulla's luggage.

Central to the Nasrudin variant is the blurring of the demarcation between wisdom and folly. After all, who but a fool would claim to listen to the Earth? Such wise Fools are a key archetype, and the Fool's journey may lead to many wonders.

The *Prose Edda*, however, gives an altogether different twist to the story. There, the Wise Woman resolves the farmers' argument by arranging a contest between them. He who can recount the greatest number of previous owners of the Land will win. The first farmer reels off an account of the seven preceding generations of farmers. But his rival proceeds to number as previous owners the animals and the plants; the worm, the mushroom, the mouse, the grass, the bee, the flower, the fox and so on for twenty generations. This second farmer, of course, wins the contest. The implication is that no human may own the Land, but may only hold it in stewardship.

These variant issues will necessarily resurface in discussion of this particular story. For now, however, the essential question is this: why is it that the central theme of the story recurs?

Land disputes are likely to be a common enough occurrence in any traditional economy for similar tales to arise in widely separated localities, or alternatively, for a travelling tale to maintain relevance upon its journeys from rural community to rural community. But the heart and life of a traditional story resides within its underlying meanings. And here the dispute over ownership of the Land runs deeper than any matter of mere property rights. Indeed, it cuts directly to the core of the human relationship with the Land.

This is a vital relationship. In one aspect, of course, this is because the Land will abide long beyond the span of a single human life, and remains the material cradle of all human society. Yet in another, more profound, aspect the Land also embraces our own Inner natures. This has been treated perceptively by other writers, such as Theodore Roszak and Alida Gersie[3]. As Roszak writes:

"Making a personality, the task that Jung called 'individuation', may be the adventure of a lifetime. But the person is anchored within a greater, universal identity. Salt remnants of ancient oceans flow through our veins, ashes of expired stars rekindle in our genetic chemistry".

At stake in our story is not only the fate of our marriage to the Outer, physical, world but also that to our own Inner selves.

It is clear that we are presented with a distinct choice of relationship. We may choose to act out the part of the farmer who regards the Land as an object that exists primarily for the benefit of himself and, secondarily, for the remainder of his human society. Alternatively, we may play the part of the farmer who, in the *Prose Edda*, understands his role as a steward for all the inhabitants of the Land, whether they be human, animal or plant. Or we may become the Wise Woman who sees, or rather hears, beyond the surface appearance of things.

It is important to appreciate the element of choice in the roles we take upon ourselves. It is possible, at the end of the story, that the farmers will abandon their shallow argument over ownership of the Land, aligning themselves with the Wise Woman's vision. Equally, they might fail to do so and continue with their inappropriate squabbling.

The winning farmer of the *Prose Edda* makes a choice to claim stewardship of the Land as opposed to outright ownership. The Wise Woman, by implication of her age and her acquired knowledge, has chosen at some time in the past to walk her particular path to awareness.

Each of us is confronted, in the normal course of our own relationship with the Land, with this set of choices. The consequences of some decisions may appear harder than others. To become the Wise Woman, certainly, suggests a difficult process of individual empowerment.

Most people choose, after all, to remain simple farmers, and to look back on previous generations of their own kind for examples of relationship with the Land. It is the easier option to stay plodding behind the plough, at war with nature and a prisoner of inheritance rather than its guardian. Marx and Engels once scorned "the idiocy of rural life"[4]; the narrowness and superstition of the peasant who remains an illiterate confined within the boundaries of his own village.

Such a peasantry still exists, albeit in declining numbers. But our modern idiocy is to remain as spiritual illiterates amidst plenty, chained by habit and convention to a human community that seeks to cut itself off from the rest of the natural world.

Consequently, for the simple farmers amongst us, the relationship with the Land constitutes a state of ongoing conflict. A rebellious and threatening Nature must be subdued by the use of whatever means come to hand. Chemical poisons are administered in liberal doses. Animals, who have at the least an equal right to tread upon the Earth with humans, may be labelled as 'vermin' in order to justify their wholesale slaughter. Nothing must stand in the way of the farmer reaping the maximum yield from the Land which he believes he owns.

Moreover, the Land is reduced to being merely the object of human power and technological domination. What does it matter if we dump our toxic wastes in the oceans and our household garbage in the woods? It all belongs to us, and we may do with it whatever we wish. The Land only retains value insofar as it is our warehouse of natural resources and material prosperity, and acts as a convenient sink for that which we have used up and discarded. This is not to suggest that the major environmental crimes of industrial corporations are of the same order as discarding an empty plastic wrapper in the countryside. But ultimately it will avail us little to heal the critical wounds inflicted upon the Land if we ignore the lesser injuries and allow them to fester. The objectification of the Land, in itself, is a barrier to the further evolution of humanity.

Such objectification is a necessary result of regarding ourselves as rightful owners of the Land. It is rather similar to treating one's own mother as a chattel to be bought or sold at will. We command her, we beat her when she disobeys, we haul her to the marketplace and sell her. Yet, like even the most downtrodden of slaves, she finds her ways of rebellion against our assumption of ownership and rule. Our efforts at subjugation are never complete, are never stringent enough. So the state of conflict with the Land goes on and on.

This has serious implications. If our own Inner nature is an integral component of the Land, then it is our own Inner selves that we beat, that we treat as a drudge, that we sell to the highest bidder. The farmer's relationship with the Land, and hence his own psyche, is a topsy-turvy one. It is as if the farmer believes that the thread turns the spinning wheel.

A true relationship with the Land involves a delicate and dynamic balance of Inner and Outer selves, not the domination of one by the other. Here lies the insight of the Wise Woman. It is her hard-earned ability to see through and hear through the apparent reality of the material plane which makes possible a lasting solution to the farmers' dispute.

The Wise Woman has the capacity to resolve the ongoing struggle against the Land, transforming it towards a more harmonious state.

Each of us, female or male, has the potential to take up the role of the Wise Woman[5], to walk the same long road to full consciousness of the Land. It is easy to flinch from the prospect of the effort involved, particularly when we live in a society dominated by the kind of quick and easy gratifications offered by, for example, fast food, soundbites, and a supply of passive entertainment courtesy of myriad television channels. The choice, however, remains before us.

The art of listening to the Land is an art that can be acquired. This is not the same as being moralistic about environmental issues. It is not the place of the Wise Woman to make moral judgements and pronouncements founded upon her own prejudices and secret desires. Rather, it is a matter of aligning or attuning oneself with the Land; hearing the heartbeat of the Earth, the whispering of the trees.

****

Exercise 6: Attunement with the Land

Most of us, even the deep city dwellers, still have some remaining access to woodland in one form or another, even if it is only a small area within an urban park. For this exercise, go there and choose a path.

As you walk along your chosen route, begin to take note of your surroundings. Look at the trees and try to identify them - it may be a good idea to have a field guide with you. Explore trees with your other senses, too. Feel their textures, smell them. You might even try tasting, but make certain beforehand that whatever you are tasting is not poisonous!

See whether you can find any peculiarities in relationships between different types of tree. Do certain trees grow near to one another? Or do certain trees tend to avoid proximity?

Try to identify the other plants that grow in the wood, too. Do any of them have value as foods or medicines? Are any of them harmful?

Look out for unique natural features. Perhaps there is an unusual rocky outcrop, or a hill of a particular shape, or a clearing that you feel drawn to. Pay some attention to the influence of humanity upon nature. Has the woodland been managed in some way? Are there signs of damage caused by humans, of littering or of dumping?

Watch, also, for signs of wildlife. For the animals who live here this is still the wildwood. Life for them remains a struggle for survival within, and often against, the natural environment. Against humans, too, at times. Think on this as you walk along the path.

Now allow your mind to move away from these physical aspects of the wood, and become aware of the subtle emotional shades that surround you. Can you feel a form of pulse, or rhythm, to the life of the wood? Does this rhythm feel different to the rhythms of urban life?

Try not to think in words, instead try to just feel and allow any images to arise. What sort of 'mood' do you feel within this woodland? Is it friendly, offhand, perhaps even hostile? Does this 'mood' alter from place to place?

When your walk is over you might find it useful to make notes of your findings. But rather than making maps, seek to fix the details of your path in your memory visually, so that you can revisit it as if replaying a video in your mind.

Over time, make a point of following the same path at different times of the year and of the day. How do the results you gain from this exercise differ according to the time and to the season?

****

Attunement, the shifting of awareness from the hubbub of everyday life to the rhythms of the Land, is the first step in learning to listen. The shift can be likened to paying attention to one particular conversation at a noisy party. The process is not necessarily an easy one. In order to grow into the role of the Wise Woman we need to relearn the values of patience and gentle persistence; values which are often lost in the bustle and ambition of the modern world, but which themselves are an aspect of attunement to the Land.

Given that the exercise in attunement has focused upon a specific place, rather than upon the concept of the Land as an abstract, it may be worth briefly discussing the importance of locality. The Wise Woman of our story is not, at least on a routine basis, concerned with matters far from home. She is connected to her home environment. She knows the Land in her immediate locality as an old friend. Her herbalism, for instance, must be based upon the plants available to her within a day's walking distance from her village.

The sense of locality remains important, even in the age of easy air travel and mail order herbalism. It is only with the aspect of the Land near to us that we can build a close and evolving relationship. We need to learn that which makes the face of the Land distinctive to us, because it is that which will be a distinctive element within our own Inner selves also.

From the process of attunement we pass to the art of actually listening to the Land. Already, while working with the attunement exercise, it may have been possible to discern, impinging upon the outer edges of consciousness, moods, thoughts or feelings that are not clearly one's own. By attunement, we start to open the ability to hear, but listening also leads to a process of interpretation.

****

Exercise 7: Listening to the Land

This exercise, again, begins with your chosen woodland. You should know it quite well now; having seen the four seasons turn through it, having learned the names (and some of the ways) of trees, plants and animals. Now return there with the intention of seeking communication.

Walk through the wood until you find a spot that feels right for you to work, where you feel physically comfortable and mentally at ease. This could be anywhere; seated under a tree, or upon a stone, or perhaps in a clearing.

Settle yourself and begin to sink into a meditative state. Slow and regulate your breathing at first. Then, however, feel for the distinctive rhythm of the wood and try to alter your breathing pattern to match this rhythm. Gradually, as you slip further and deeper into meditation, sense yourself becoming more and more attuned to the wood that surrounds you.

Feel roots growing from the base of your spine, visualise them reaching down and gripping hold of the Earth. Feel the sensation of sap being drawn into these roots, then up and into your body. Keep your breathing, all this time, synchronised with the pulse of the woods around you. Know that you have become part of the wood.

Be aware, now, of the feeling of the woodland seeping into your stilled consciousness. The thoughts of the wood are most likely to shape themselves in your mind as images. Allow these to flow by, holding onto each image for just a few moments before letting it go. Remember that you are listening, not conversing.

Stay in this receptive state for as long as you feel comfortable. When you are ready, slowly return your breathing to its normal rate. Open your eyes. As soon as possible, write down notes of all that you can remember from the flow of images. It is also wise to leave some form of offering in thanks for all that you have received; perhaps a Blessing, or a little food for the woodland animals.

With some thought, this exercise (and the preceding exercise) may be adapted for use in environments other than the woods.

****

Actually making use of all that we learn from the act of listening to the Land may seem to be problematic. We are unfortunate to be living in a society which recognises only human voices - and few enough of those. To listen to other voices, such as that of the Land, will bring us to be viewed in much the same light as Mulla Nasrudin. Some will see us as wise, but more often we will be regarded as foolish.

Still, the Fool, as in the Tarot trumps, is only at the beginning of a long journey. A willingness to study symbolism - including the collective symbolism around us and the personal symbolism to be found within our dreams - will help to guide us in interpreting the language of imagery with which the Land speaks to us, and in developing our personal relationship with the Land.

For the time being, we need simply note the value of being discriminatory in whom we speak to of our first steps on the path of the Wise Woman. To be conscious, also, that this path is one that ultimately is of service to the Land, and not of mastery.

The Green Ladies of One Tree Hill

There was once a farmer who owned a great deal of land and who was very wealthy. That wealth was quite remarkable, to tell the truth, because the land was not good but somehow it yielded the most marvellous harvests year upon year, the farmer's cows gave the sweetest milk and from his sheep came the finest wool. As if by miracle, the farmer prospered against all the odds.

There was a reason for this. Near to one edge of the farmer's land there was a hill, which was never ploughed and upon which no animal was ever set to graze. On the very top of this hill there stood three tall, majestic beech trees.

It was a place mostly avoided, for some folk said that on certain nights eerie music could be heard from the hill, and that in the moonlight three Green Ladies could be seen dancing around and between the silver trees. Yet every year, without fail, on Midsummer Eve the farmer climbed the hill and laid a posy of wild flowers at the foot of each beech tree.

Now, the farmer had three sons, all of them fine, strong lads. As he was growing older, and knew that he was going to die in time, he often called the three sons together and advised them as to how they should run the farm once he was gone. There was one thing he always reminded them of before he sent them on their way again.

"*Remember*", he said, "*that all our luck lies upon the hill, and do not forget to honour the trees each year*".

Some years passed by and the old farmer passed into the next world. The big farm was divided up in the customary way. The oldest of the three sons inherited the largest portion; the middle brother inherited most of the rest. The youngest found himself with the slightest parcel of poor land just at the base of the hill, with only one skinny cow and a tumbledown cottage.

Well, the youngest son set to work with the little he had inherited. He worked hard, and he remembered his father's words. Each Midsummer Eve he walked up the hill and laid a posy of wild flowers at the foot of each tree. Soon his little plot was prospering, there were surplus crops to sell at market, the cow was fat and contented and giving milk by the bucketful, and the cottage was put into good repair. On moonlit nights the strange music played on the hill and the three Green Ladies danced.

The other two brothers, however, either forgot or ignored their father's advice. Their shares of the land were doing far less well. It was not long before the eldest noticed how successfully his youngest brother was faring, and saw him climbing the hill on Midsummer Eve. The jealousy and resentment began to boil up inside him, until at last they overflowed. So one day he called on the youngest brother.

"*I see your plot of land is giving good harvests. I also see you on the hill, lurking among the trees*", said the elder brother.

"I work hard and I visit the hill from time to time", said the younger.

"*No longer*", said the elder angrily, "t*he hill is my land and you are trespassing. You stay away from there, or I'll call the law onto you. Anyway, I'm going to cut down the trees and use their wood in building my new barn*".

Sure enough, the following day he came back with a crowd of his servants and labourers, most of them carrying new-sharpened axes, and a train of carts to take away the trees once they had been cut down. But the servants and labourers, when they came to the foot of the hill, remembered the times they had heard the music and seen the dancers. One after another, they laid down their axes, dreading what might happen should they obey their master.

The eldest brother was beside himself with fury. He seized hold of the nearest axe and set off angrily up the hill alone. When he reached the summit he hefted the axe in both his hands and aimed a fierce blow at the nearest of the beech trees.

All heard the cry of the tree as the sharp edge of the axe bit home. It sounded like the scream of a woman. Again and again the axe struck, again and again the tree shrieked; until at last the cries stopped and the tree, with a mighty cracking sound, toppled over.

But even in its death the tree had its revenge, for it came crashing down directly onto the man who had felled it. There was a terrible silence. When the eldest brother's servants came up the hill they found him lying there stone dead, half buried beneath the great trunk of the fallen beech tree.

The carts were brought up, and both the body of the man and the body of the tree were carried away in them. Stories were told of how the Green Lady had taken a life in her own dying; and on moonlit nights the strange music was still to be heard, although only two Green Ladies could now be seen dancing upon the hill.

The middle brother inherited all that there was to inherit, once the burying was done. The youngest brother kept his own small plot, which flourished as it always had. Each Midsummer Eve he still climbed the hill and left a posy of wild flowers at the foot of both of the trees.

But the middle brother's farm fared less well. Profits were few and were long in coming. It seemed as though he was working hard for little reward, while his brother had nothing but good luck. Envy and self-righteous anger were spawned inside him like twin cancers, and with every day that passed they grew bigger, stronger and more poisonous.

At last they could be contained no longer. The middle brother went to call on the younger.

"You are doing well for someone little better than a common farmhand", he said, *"and I still see you on the hill from time to time"*.

"I work hard and I am lucky", the younger brother replied, *"and it is true that I visit the hill when I feel that I must"*.

"You'll stay away from the hill from now on. It's my land. I'm going to cut down the trees, and use their timber to build a fence that will keep you off", snarled the middle brother.

He was as good as his word. Not a night and a day had passed before he came back with a great troop of his servants, every man bearing a sharp axe, and with many carts to bear away the timber. However, as soon as they came close to the hill and understood what was expected of them, the servants threw down their tools and would go no further. The middle brother railed and cursed, to no avail. At last, maddened and exasperated, he snatched up one of the axes himself and strode purposefully towards the two beech trees on the hilltop.

Without a moment's thought or hesitation he laid the axe to one of the trees. At his first blow all heard the tree cry out, and the sound it made was like the scream of a woman. Again and again the axe cut in, and at each and every blow the tree screamed. Until, at last, the tree gave a final groan and fell to lie still upon the ground.

The middle brother rested his axe and turned to call his servants to him. Even as he did so, there was another sharp "Crack!" as a bough broke from the last standing tree and fell, striking him hard upon his head. When the servants reached him they found him sprawled, dead, across the body of the tree that he had cut down.

Both bodies, that of the man and that of the tree, were taken away solemnly in the carts. Countryfolk whispered of how the fallen Green Lady had been avenged by her surviving sister. None of them would come venturing near to the hill, which they now said was either haunted or accursed.

As for the youngest brother, he naturally inherited all the land that his father had owned. Each Midsummer Eve he climbed the hill and laid down a posy of wild flowers for the sole remaining tree. Both the farm and the farmer prospered.

The hill is still there, and to this day a solitary beech tree stands upon it. Hence it is known as One Tree Hill. Local people may tell you that on moonlit nights there is heard from the hill the plaintive sound of a strange, melancholy music; and that dancing about the hilltop and the tree you might then see a lone Green Lady.

****

There has always been something special in the contact between humans and trees.

During the Seventeenth Century, the Maharajah of Jodhpur sent many servants into the forests near to the Bishnoi village of Khejadali, in order to gather timber for the building of a new palace. But to the Bishnoi, the trees were sacred.

A local woman, Amritadevi, heard the sound of axes as they began to bite into the trees of the forest. Swiftly she ran to one of the trees and tried to protect it with her own body from the Maharajah's men. She was immediately cut down by their axes, and she died.

Nevertheless, other Bishnoi villagers followed her example. Women and children sought to defend their trees, as the men were away working. By the end of that day, more than 363 people lay dead. When news of this slaughter reached the ears of the Maharajah, he was so appalled that he ordered an end to the tree felling.

Today, most of Rajasthan is a treeless desert. Only the Bishnoi people, there, live amidst greenery[1].

In Celtic cultures, the trees were key to magic, myth and ritual. In ancient Ireland, five sacred trees in particular upheld the Land, and heavy punishments were laid upon anyone who felled or damaged one of the seven "Chieftain trees" - oak, holly, ash, hazel, apple, pine and yew; while lighter fines awaited those who harmed other trees and shrubs[2]. Contemporary writers, recorded that the oak was central to the beliefs and practices of the Druids.

The old Greek story of 'The King and the Oak' tells how the felling of a sacred grove brought ruin down upon an entire kingdom[4].

Still, today, in the British Isles some trees may be seen hung with rags upon their branches, as offerings for healing and of praise. Other peoples, among them some native Americans, Indians, the inhabitants of the Mediterranean region, the Japanese and the Tibetans, have the same or similar traditions of dressing trees.

In African traditional societies, the tree is often at the very heart of community, as both meeting place and sacred enclosure.

The story of 'The Green Ladies of One Tree Hill' is drawn from this rich stream of lore and ancestral relationship. It carries the wisdom, from teller to listener, that has always surrounded trees as guardians of the Land, as its symbols, and as a channel of communication and con-nectedness to the environment as a whole.

But there is a second strand of tradition that winds through and around this tale. The Green Ladies are tree spirits, creatures of the Otherworld who live alongside humanity, dwellers in the same space but upon a different plane. Here, they are bound directly to a certain location, the farm that prospers with their protection and favour.

They require little, in a material sense, in return. Yet the simple offering made each Midsummer Eve represents something more significant than a material sacrifice; it demonstrates the continuance of respect and an awareness of the sacred nature of the Land and its inhabitants, flowing from generation to generation.

****

Exercise 8: Working with the trees

In our own modern society, the relationship between humans and trees has, by and large, fallen into a state of disrepair. The intent of this exercise is to begin to restore the bonds, on an individual level at least.

Initially you need to start learning to identify the various types of tree, and here a field guide would be an asset. Some trees will probably be familiar to you already - oak, beech, birch, holly and so on. You should find that every individual tree has a "feel" of its own, this could be thought of as the "personality" of the tree. Now search for one that you sense has almost human aspects to that personality. Such trees will often appear to stand out in some indefinable way from others, or from the landscape around them.

When you have located your tree, go up close to it. Quietly try to pick up impressions of how the tree itself is feeling. Is it happy or sad? Comfortable with your presence? Does it feel lively and energetic, or withdrawn? Open to contact or dark, perhaps even brooding? This is easier to write about than to actually do! So you may not obtain instant answers to your questions, but the key is to be patient - gentle perseverance rather than an intrusive pushiness should eventually bring results. Now place the palms of your hands against the trunk, close your eyes, and feel for a "pulse" just as though feeling for the pulse of a human being.

You might also find it valuable to dowse the tree you are studying. A pendulum can be used to keep a check on the tree's energy levels, while L-rods will indicate the extent of any energy field around the tree.

It's important to carry on working with the same tree right through the cycle of the year. Try to work out how the tree is affected by different times and seasons, by different phases of the Moon, and by different kinds of weather.

As soon as you have started working with one type of tree you can go on to begin with others as well. Some trees are particularly darkly aspected - examples are holly, ivy, yew, blackthorn and elder - and are best not worked with until you have acquired some experience with those that are less harsh. Look out for apparent affinities between the various species of tree. Gradually you will see a picture building up of the Inner, magical, characteristics of the various trees; their seasonal cycles, moods, partnerships and even rivalries.

Do remember to leave an offering each time that you work with a tree, in return for the knowledge you have gained. Leave a Blessing, written onto a strip of cloth and tied to a branch, or perhaps a little wine or bread. You may even prefer, like the characters in our story, to leave a small posy at the foot of the tree.

****

Too often, the trees around us are sorry specimens, neglected, and surrounded with brick and concrete. It seems to be a mark of how far we have fallen from the conceptualisation of the sacred landscape, that usually our trees are valued only for their timber or for their decorative worth in our towns and parks.

Consistently working with the exercise above should begin to deepen individual bonds with the trees. This is not merely a matter of sentimental attachment. The trees are the most powerful and individual of the plant inhabitants of the Land. As such, they are both thoroughly rooted within the processes of the Land, and capable of relating to and of communicating with human levels of consciousness.

To some degree, it is possible that such communication may be opened up without deliberate effort, as progress is made in creating a relationship with particular trees.

The Earth Will Have Its Own

Long, long ago there lived a widow, who had but the one son. As he grew up he learned to look all around him, and what he saw was this. The other children of his village had fathers, but he did not. The oxen that drew the plough, the wild beasts, the birds, even the lowly insects crawling upon the Earth, all had fathers, but he did not.

"Mother", asked the boy, *"why is it that I do not have a father of my own?"*

"Your father is dead, long dead", answered his mother sadly.

"Will he ever come back to us?"

"No, your father will never come back", his mother replied, *"but in time we will go to him. Nobody can escape death, we too must die in our turn and be buried in the bosom of the Earth".*

At this, the young boy grew angry. *"I did not ask for my life"*, he said, *"so why must it be taken away from me? I will go from here, and seek out a place where there is no death".*

His mother argued with him, she cajoled, she begged, but all to no avail. Try as she might, she could no more keep him from going out into the world and looking for a land without death than she could hold back the night with her two hands. In spite of her, the boy set out upon his wanderings.

Year after year, he walked over the whole face of the Earth. At every place he came to he asked, "*Is there death here?*" He always met with the same answer, "*Yes, yes, there is death here*". He came to be twenty years old, yet still he had not discovered the Land of the Ever-Living.

Then, one day, he was walking across a field when he saw standing before him a stag, whose great branching antlers grew so high that they pierced the clouds and disappeared from view. The youth marvelled at the sight of these antlers. He approached the stag and asked, "*In the name of the Creator of the world, tell me, is there a place upon this Earth where there is no death?*"

"*I am the messenger of God and I fulfil His will*", the stag answered, "*I shall live until my antlers touch the heavens, but then I too must die. If you wish, you may remain with me until the day of my death; you will want for nothing*".

"*No, I will either live forever or not at all*", replied the youth, "*Else I could have stayed safely at home, without undertaking this pilgrimage of mine at all*".

He left the stag in the field with these words and continued on his travels. Through deserts and across mountains he walked, over plains and seas and through dense forests he travelled.

At last he came to a great crack in the Earth. He looked down over the rim and it seemed to yawn bottomless, so that he thought it must be the very entrance to Hell itself.

All around the mouth of this chasm, great rocks reared and thrust up towards the sky. On the peak of one of these a huge black raven sat motionless. The youth called out to it, "*In the name of the Creator of the world, tell me, is there a place upon this Earth where there is no death?*"

"*I am the messenger of God and I fulfil His will*", said the raven, "*I will live until the day that I have grown so large that I fill up this abyss. If you wish, you may remain with me until that day, when I must die. You will want for nothing*".

"*No, I will either live forever or not at all*", responded the youth, "*Otherwise I could have stayed at home with my mother and not undertaken this quest*".

Leaving these words with the raven, he went on his way. He walked for years, until he came to the brink of a great ocean, without meeting anybody else. The land seemed to be deserted, but he saw something glinting in the distance. He started towards it, and as he came near he saw that it was a house built entirely of glass, that shone in the sunlight.

At first the youth could see no doors, but when he examined the walls more closely he saw that a line was marked upon the glass. When he pressed his hand on this line, the house opened up for him. Within, there lay a maiden so beautiful that the Sun itself was jealous of her, and dimmed sullenly as she appeared. The youth, too, was astonished by her beauty. In awe, he approached her.

"In the name of the Creator of this world, tell me, is there a place upon this Earth where there is no death?"

"Such a place does not exist", said the maiden, *"but why seek it when you can stay here with me?"*

"I did not leave my home to find you", the youth said, *"I set out to search for the land where there is no death"*.

"Alas", responded the maiden, *"your quest is in vain. You will never find the Land of the Ever-Living, the Earth will have its own. But tell me, if you are able, how old am I?"*

For a long time the youth gazed at the maiden. The longer he looked, the more enchanted he was. At last he forgot both life and death.

"You cannot be above fifteen years old", he said.

"You are wrong", said the maiden, *"for I was made on the first day of Creation. Today I am just as I was then. I will always be so, for my name is Beauty. Perhaps you could have remained with me until the last day of Time, but you are not worthy of such immortality. Even everlasting life would grow distasteful to you"*.

Yet the youth promised that it would not be so. He vowed that he would never act against her will, to always stay at her side. Eventually the maiden relented.

Henceforth the youth lived in the glass house by the ocean with Beauty. Years flew by, one after another, faster and faster it seemed to him; until he thought of them as no more than seconds. The Earth was changing without cease, but in the glass house the youth knew nothing of this, and Beauty remained always the same.

Thus a century passed, then a second, and a third. Soon the youth began to long for his home. He found himself wondering, more and more, what had become of his mother, of his childhood friends and acquaintances.

One day he said to the maiden, *"I must return to my home, if only for one day, to see my mother and my friends"*.

"There is no use in going home", said the maiden, *"By now their bones will have become dust, and that dust scattered by the four winds"*.

"You are speaking nonsense", the youth interjected angrily, *"I have only lived with you for a short time, why should they be dead already?"*

"I told you on your first day with me", the maiden said softly, *"that you would not be worthy of everlasting life. Do as you wish. Take these three apples with you and when you come to your home, eat them"*.

The youth took the three apples and left the maiden, journeying homewards. He came to the abyss, but the raven had filled that huge chasm and was dead. He came to where the stag stood in the field, but that too was dead and the heavens were supported upon its antlers. At last he entered his own village.

The youth met nobody that he knew. He asked the whereabouts of his mother; only one elderly couple could tell him that there had once been, according to an old tradition, a woman of that name. But that had been many centuries past and her son could no longer be living.

Not one person would believe his tale, that he really was the son of that woman. The simple peasant folk thought that he must be a messenger from God, so that they all followed him as he wandered here and there through the village. He came to the place where his mother's house had once stood. Ruined, broken walls were smothered by moss and nettles. With sorrow and bitterness he remembered his mother and his childhood, all lost.

Then he recalled the apples that the maiden had given him. He ate the first of them, and a white beard fell from his chin, covering his chest. He ate the second, and his knees gave way as his strength forsook him. He was so weak and frail that he had to ask one of the boys gathered about to give him the third apple. As soon as he had eaten it, his soul flew free from his body. The Earth will have its own.

The people of the village buried him there, and his grave may still be seen.

****

Remaking our personal relationship with the natural world brings us closer to an intimate awareness of the rhythms and cycles of the Land. Night alternates with day, the four seasons come circling around again and again. Because we, too, are a part of the Land we begin to grow conscious of these same progressions within ourselves, of how we relate to them, mostly in terms of our consciousness but perhaps also in the changes we feel in our physical bodies.

Foremost among these natural cycles is the greatest of them all, the cycle of life and death. Death, indeed, is all around us in nature. It is in the food chain, it is in the limitations with which the Land itself encloses life and the expansion of life. It is in the dark and barren times of Winter.

Fear of this death, as well, seems to lurk behind our own individual lives at every step we take, like some doomy shadow. It is a part of us, it goes with us wherever we go, yet we would cast it off if we could.

Like the hero of the story, we all tend to wander from place to place in search of a land where there is no death, even if only in our fantasies. Tales of immortality, or which hold out the hope of immortality, have held humanity in their fascination through history, even when eternity is blackened by darkness and horror, as in the legends of vampires. It is interesting that such stories seem to gain in popularity when humanity is living through the times of greatest uncertainty. Is it possible that this tendency is an element in the current resurgence of the vampire as cultural icon?[1]

However, in reality, we cannot evade the second law of thermodynamics. Because we are physically rooted upon this material plane, it is simply not possible for us to dodge the approach of physical death, which must come sooner or later. The Earth will have its own.

This is an important sentence, a key to open the meaning of the story. The elements of which we are made are taken from the Earth. They must, in time, be returned to the Earth. There is a debt that must always be repaid. Perhaps we can expand the meaning of the Earth to embrace the Land as a whole, in which case we discover a new, further layer of significance to this.

Certainly our physical bodies are ours only on loan, as it were; it is possible also that a part of our consciousness must be given up at the point of death, given up to the collective entity that surrounds us like an ocean.

There is a chant that I have heard, a song which, I am told, originates from a native American tradition:

> *The river is flowing, flowing and growing,*
> *The river is flowing, back to the sea.*
> *Mother Earth carry me, a child I will always be,*
> *Mother Earth carry me, down to the sea.*[2]

In this there is an acceptance that progression, growth, the long and hard process of individuation, must lead us ultimately back to fusion. Yet the song is not a message of despair, rather it looks toward this future wholeheartedly and peacefully.

Both physically and psychologically, much of human history has entailed a struggle against the inevitability of death. It is seen as the great oblivion, the blotting out of all that we are. No wonder those with sufficient wealth and power to do so have raised such great monuments to preserve their own memories in the minds of those who come after - it is a final railing against the march of destiny.

Futile, too. But those who have remained close to the Land, those who are integrated with the Land, do not experience the same shattering and demoralising sense of futility. As you live with the passing, spiralling seasons of the Land you should also become aware of their truth, the hope held out to all that is mortal. That which dies in Winter is reborn in Spring. That which withers in the darkness will sprout and flower again with the renewed light.

So that the fusion with the greater waters of the collective Unconscious, with the awesome totality of the Land, is no longer a finality towards which we race downhill but one season in the ever-turning cycle of seasons.

****

Exercise 9: The Cycle of Life, Death and Rebirth

What follows is the outline for a cycle of ritual work that may help to bring you into alignment with, and Inner awareness of, the great wheel of life, death and rebirth.

I have deliberately limited myself to giving only the very briefest of outlines; so that you are free to embellish and adapt according to your own level of experience, Tradition if any, and personal inclinations. These rituals are not intended as a substitute for the Seasonal Rites of any Tradition which you might follow, but may supplement them if properly and carefully integrated.

February 1st, Imbolc - Emergence into new life
Wear white, or work naked. Form a simple Circle (see Appendix). Spend some time quietly meditating on an Inner name for yourself. This is not a permanent "magical name", it is only intended to be temporary, lasting through this cycle of rituals; and if you wish, it may refer to a particular aim or project. When you have found a name that suits you, state your intent to adopt it as your Inner name, and "seal" it with a sprinkling of salt water. Plant a seed into a pot of earth. If you possess an Ivy crown from the preceding year (see the ritual for Samhain), you will need to cast this onto flowing water.

May 1st, Beltaine - Maturation

Men wear red, women wear green. Form a simple Circle. Light a candle. Say, "*As this candle fills the Circle with light, so may my life shine within the Land*". Meditate quietly for a time on the theme of this ritual. From a container of coloured ribbons (there should be plenty of different colours) draw one ribbon. With what quality do you associate the colour? Think on how this may relate to your chosen Inner name. Say, "*I will seek for the flowering of this (quality) as the woods and the fields flower through the light and warmth of Summer*".

August 1st, Lughnasadh - Harvest

Men wear red, women wear green. Form a simple Circle. How have you grown and learned? What might the consequences be? Say, "*In the time of harvest I will gather the fruits of all that I have planted, for good or for ill; in full knowledge that both are part of the gaining of wisdom*". Eat either bread or cake that should contain at least a part of whatever plant you have grown from the seed planted at Imbolc. Meditate quietly on the theme of this ritual.

October 31st, Samhain - Death

Wear white, or work naked. You should also wear a circular crown made with Ivy. Form a simple Circle. Take some time to write a short "Death Poem" that sums up the cycle that is ending. Say, "*As I don this crown of Ivy I sacrifice the name that I took at the birth of Spring. And I pass into the darkness of Winter knowing the cycle of life, death and rebirth; knowing that Spring will come again*". Bury in the earth the coloured ribbon from Beltaine.

The Wildwood King

There was once a king, and he had three daughters. Of these, two were neither beautiful nor were they ugly. The youngest, on the other hand, was as beautiful as beautiful can be. When any man came to seek the hand of the oldest daughter, and so become the king's heir himself, he would straight away fall in love with the youngest girl. The same happened to every man who came for the second daughter. Thus none of the three girls could manage to get married.

In time, the two older daughters grew so exasperated that they hatched a plot against their beautiful sister. One morning they each went to their father the king, separately, and told him that they had both dreamed the same dream. They claimed that they had foreseen that their sister would elope with a common soldier, thus bringing disgrace down upon the proud heads of the royal family.

The king flew into a terrible and deadly rage. In his anger he summoned to him his most trusted general and gave a dreadful order. The general was to take the king's youngest daughter out into the woods of the wildwood king and there, deep among the trees, he was to cut her down with his sword.

So it was that the very next day they went walking together in the woods of the wildwood king, the general and the maiden. They wandered further and further, following unfamiliar paths that led towards the very heart of the woods. After a time, the maiden began to feel uneasy.

"*I have walked far enough today*", she said to the general, "*Let's go home now*".

"*Oh no*", said the general, "*I am sorry, but I have been ordered to kill you here in the woods*".

"*Why would anybody want to kill me?*" asked the young girl, thoroughly bewildered.

"*I have been given my orders by your father, the King*", said the general, unsheathing his sword and raising it for the fatal strike.

But the poor maiden was so shocked and so frightened that suddenly the general, loyal to the king as he was, took pity upon her. The death blow never fell. Instead the general turned the maiden free in the woods; although he took her clothes and as he returned to the palace he soaked them in the blood of a butchered lamb, so that the king would believe that the wicked deed had been carried through.

Meanwhile, the girl remained in the woods, wandering and weeping, afraid of her fate. For she had heard folk tell stories of the wildwood king. Of how he lived in the woods that were his domain, alone and terrifying. Of how he slew and ate anybody who chanced to cross his path. Eventually she could neither walk nor cry any longer. She sat down, allowing the tears to dry at last, then curled herself up in a hollow tree trunk and fell soundly asleep.

The following morning, the wildwood king was out hunting. As he pursued a wounded stag along the woodland paths, he passed the hollow tree within which the maiden lay, and he saw her there. The wildwood king was moved by her beauty. The fleeing stag was forgotten and for a time he watched over her as she slept.

At last he awakened her. The maiden started, suddenly terrified, recalling the tales. But rather than devouring her the wildwood king smiled, saying, "*Do not be afraid. Come with me and live in my house*".

At first the maiden was hesitant, cautious as she was of the wildwood king's dark reputation. Yet he was so gentle and so kind with her. She accepted his offer, following him to his house in the depths of the woods, where he lived a solitary life; hunting alone each day and never seeing another living soul. The maiden began to keep the house and the wildwood king swiftly grew to love her as his own daughter.

One morning as she rose from her bed, and sat to braid her long hair by the window, a brightly plumed parrot flew down and alighted upon the window ledge. It cocked its head to one side and called out:

> "*In vain are you pretty and neat,*
> *You will become the forest king's meat*".

When she heard these words, the girl began to cry. Soon after, the wildwood king returned home from hunting. Finding her so distressed, he asked, "*What is the matter?*" Then the maiden told him what the parrot had said to her.

"*I shall tell you how you should reply to him*", said the wildwood king. He told her to respond with this rhyme:

> *"Parrot, parrot, hear this ban,*
> *Your feathers for my fan,*
> *Your meat is for my pan,*
> *Your master will become my man!"*

Sure enough, the very next morning the parrot returned, settling on the maiden's window ledge again. It fixed her with a beady eye and called out:

> *" In vain are you pretty and neat,*
> *You will become the forest king's meat".*

Instead of bursting into tears, this time the maiden turned and called back in reply:

> *"Parrot, parrot, hear this ban,*
> *Your feathers for my fan,*
> *Your meat is for my pan,*
> *Your master will become my man!"*

At this, the parrot was beside itself with temper. In spite, it shook its body with such fury that fully half its gaudy feathers fell out and onto the ground.

It so happened that this parrot belonged to another king who lived nearby. When he saw his unfortunate bird come home half-bald he immediately summoned his servants together and asked, *"Who is plucking out the parrot's feathers?"*

The servants responded, *"Each morning your parrot, sire, flies off towards the house of the wildwood king and later comes home plucked".*

The king said, *"Tomorrow morning I shall follow through the woods, and find out for myself what is going on".*

That is what he did. On horseback he followed the direction of his parrot's flight, deep into the woods. When he came to the house of the wildwood king he saw the most beautiful maiden, sitting at an open window, braiding her hair. The parrot flew down and sat upon her window ledge. It called out:

"In vain are you pretty and neat,
You will become the forest king's meat".

The maiden turned and called back:

"Parrot, Parrot, hear this ban,
Your feathers for my fan,
Your meat is for my pan,
Your master will become my man!"

The parrot was so angry that it shook itself violently and all its feathers fell out onto the ground.

The king, however, was stricken with love for the maiden. He waited until the wildwood king returned from the hunt, then went to him and asked humbly for the girl's hand in marriage.

The wildwood king gave his permission gladly, although it grieved his own heart to be separated from his adopted daughter. That very day the maiden left with her new bridegroom, leaving the wildwood king alone once more in the heart of the woods.

Among the many guests at the wedding banquet was the maiden's own royal father, who sank upon one knee before her and asked forgiveness for his own folly and wickedness, and for all the suffering he had caused at the prompting of her two sisters.

And you ask what became of the parrot? Pink and bald as he was, he slunk off into the woods in shame and was never seen again.

****

Our first hint of the Wildwood King himself is darkly aspected. His face is the face of fear, that of a monster lurking in the forest and waiting to devour the hapless traveller. At least, this is the initial perception. For the other characters in the story, the mysterious Wildwood King becomes the embodiment of a dangerous and potentially destructive Nature, as they superimpose their own Shadows onto his image.

The environment of the wildwood is itself perceived as an adversary to the orderly realms of humanity. These are so orderly, in fact, that even a King's daughter may face personal extinction if it is as much as thought that she could flout the conventions and laws of the day. Thus she is taken off into the forest, for she has aligned herself with the forces of disorder and chaos which the wildwood is believed to represent.

The maiden herself, ironically, still personifies this deep alienation from Nature. Her own terror of her situation breaks its boundaries, so that she wanders weeping, lost and helpless, among the trees. This contradiction in the maiden's situation, the core of injustice in her circumstances, is designed to invoke our sympathy for her plight. She still, by virtue of her entire upbringing and experience, regards herself as a part of the civilisation which opposes itself to the mysterious and alien environment of the wildwood. Yet that same culture sees her as a part of the very forest that she herself fears, and has outcast her as such.

When the expected confrontation comes with the Wildwood King, the maiden is not devoured, contrary to her own terrors and the imaginations of those who have rejected her. Before meeting the Wildwood King she had perceived him as a creature of Darkness, but at this point it is his Light aspect that is revealed to her. From here on the maiden's experience of the forest is no longer a fearful trauma, but a relationship in which the wildwood, through the intervention of the Wildwood King himself, becomes her ally and her protector.

For the essence of the Wildwood King's bond to his own domain is that the King and his realm are one and the same. Historically, this ancient and profound correspondence survived in the belief that human monarchs were the personification of the kingdoms that they ruled. Concepts of "marriage" to the realm and to the Land itself have always been at the heart of the rituals of kingship.

We may draw further insights into the nature of the Wildwood King from the spiritual traditions that he may have sprung from. The King can be seen as a form of the Horned God, a deity as old as human societies. There are several indications of this. The Horned God presents himself as a God of the woods and of wild Nature; is Lord and patron of the hunt; and is dually aspected as both God of Light, life and Summer, and as God of Darkness, death and Winter[1]. The similarities of the Wildwood King are striking. He is, of course, ruler of the woods, he is a hunter, and he has both Light and Dark aspects to his character - he comes to the maiden's aid, but the suggestion that he might also be capable of devouring unwary travellers is never rejected.

The exile of the Wildwood King from human culture can therefore be understood as our alienation from all that the Horned God personifies. In particular, the masculine element in Nature is perceived as a power to be negated, a force that is nothing but Darkness and danger, to be driven out from consciousness. Nature is only accepted if deprived of wildness and, in our psychology, feminised. This is a significant step, because in the terms of our culture the feminine is prone to be subjugated, tamed.

If this attitude to Nature applies also to its deeper aspect, to the Land, then some illuminating parallels may be drawn. There is, to begin with, a societal conflict with the raw and non-rational aspects of consciousness. Yet it is these very forces, the fertilising power of the Horned God, which may awaken our consciousness to its full potential.

Mention was made earlier, during discussion of the King's role in the story of 'The Harp on the Water', of the question of polarity. Put straightforwardly, polarity entails the balancing and inter-relationship of opposite energies - light and dark, male and female.

There is, however, a danger of oversimplification in this definition because, for example, masculine energies contain within themselves the seed of the feminine, and vice versa[2].

Our awareness of the feminine pole of the Land is, generally speaking, of the gentle and subjected variety of the female. Untamed, She is deeper and more powerful, and contact with Her, the development of a relationship with Her, both releases the full power of the Unconscious and opens the path to the sacred marriage to the Land[3]. However, the route towards that bond lies first through contact with the Wildwood King, who holds the domains of the Land in his safekeeping.

Exercise 10: Meeting the Wildvood King

For some time, now, you will have been exploring your woodland; working with the trees and the plants, learning the paths, taking into yourself the sense and the atmosphere of the Land. It is time to connect at a deeper level.

Sit and settle into a meditative state of consciousness. Regulate your breathing and begin to withdraw from the outer world. See before your Inner vision a door, of heavy wood and slightly arched at the top, but without any visible handle or lock on this side. Wait patiently until you hear a sound as of a key turning, and the door opens of its own accord, slowly and gently.

Beyond the open door you can see the beginning of your customary path through the woodland. Stand, and step across the threshold. Pause on the pathway for a while. Hear the sounds of the woods around you in the rustling of small animals through the undergrowth, the singing of birds, the creaking of tree branches and the whisper of leaves in the wind. Note the season of the year and the time of day.

Now start to walk. Follow your normal route, which by this point should be familiar to you, with the same awareness and observation that you would maintain if you were walking through these woods upon the material plane.

It is not possible to predict what you will see, or exactly what manner of Inner World beings you are likely to meet.

Much depends upon the nature of the woodland through which you are travelling, upon the individual natures of its denizens, and also upon your own personal level of development. This Inner journey is very much a personal quest. What is important is to retain in mind the object of the exercise, which is to seek out and meet with the Wildwood King himself.

Ask those you meet if they will lead you to him, or bring him to you. And remember to be polite!

It is almost certain that you will have to make this journey into the Inner woodland more than once. In fact, the more it is used, the more your relationship with your wood will evolve; especially if, at the same time, your material relationship with the woodland is maintained.

Do not stay too long on the other side of the door, especially at first. You will feel yourself being "pulled" to return; do not resist this, but retrace your steps to the beginning of the path, having taken your leave of any Inner beings that you may be with. You will see the door again, and it will open before you to reveal your room and the chair in which you were originally seated. Step through the door, and sit down in your chair once more. The door closes, quietly, behind you and you hear again the sound of a key turning, locking the door in place.

Return to your full everyday consciousness, slowly and gently. Be sure to "ground" yourself, a good way is to eat a biscuit and sip a hot drink, and record in writing the details of your journey.

****

The precise manner in which contact may be established with the Wildwood King in the first place, and the ways in which a relationship with him subsequently develops, must be largely left to subjective experience.

The figure of the Wildwood King does have an objective reality within our collective psyche, but this is filtered through individual awareness so that our own meeting with him is a personal affair.

Such a connection with the Wildwood King can go some distance towards rebalancing our relationship with the Land itself, at least on the individual level. This form of personal growth is neither isolating nor self-centred. Its effects will seep into the collective experience of the Land at the level of the Unconscious, contributing to the raising of humanity to a higher, more evolved consciousness.

Yet even so, our journey through the forest is not over. We have been led into the heart of the Land, but below the surface lie other forces, dormant, waiting for the dawn.

Where the Sleepers Wait

I suppose that in every street in every town there is one family with a bad reputation, the one house in the street that everybody skirts carefully around, and through the front windows of which nobody ever risks a glance. Yet our street could win the prize in a contest of bad reputations.

On the corner there is a big, rundown old house with a big yard at the back, and in front there are always several old heaps that might still be just recognisable as trucks and vans, each of them piled high with a tottering assortment of junk, everything from flearidden old mattresses to car parts. In that house lives the worst family of no-good rogues to be found anywhere between South London and the English Channel, the Callots.

It's anybody's guess how many Callots there are; it has been said that they are more like a tribe than a family. They seem to teem everywhere, and they are up to their necks in any dodgy business or crookedness that brings in hard cash, from dealing in scrap to fixing up cars on the cheap and selling them on, from working in the fields through the summer while still signing on the dole to (some say) a little house-breaking on the side.

Maybe the worst of the whole clan of Callots, aside from his father, was always the eldest of the sons, Kit Callot. A brawny foul-mouthed braggart, Kit Callot, broad as he is tall, and with a fondness for using his big fists to settle even the slightest of disagreements. This story is about him.

It so happened that the Callots somehow or other came into possession of a horse; nobody ever knew exactly how this came about, but they seemed eager enough to be parted from it. The horse was no thoroughbred, but was sturdy and quick all the same, and the Callots soon had a buyer. Some family out on the more rural fringes of the Medway Towns, with more money than scruples.

So one day the reins of the horse were put into the hands of Kit Callot, and he was sent off to walk the horse to its new owners, the Callots not having a better way of transporting it. A simple enough task, you might think, for it was not a particularly long journey and Kit was easily big enough and strong enough to maintain control of the animal.

But then, Kit was never the most reliable worker. The day was bright, hot and dusty, so that Kit had walked no further than one of the local pubs when a terrible thirst came upon him and he just had to stop off for a while. He tied the horse to a tree outside for safety, then slipped away inside where the shade was cool and the beer flowed without the hindrance of closing times.

By the time he came out again the sun was setting over in the west and he was more than slightly the worse for wear, but the horse still waited for him and he reasoned that now the long walk would be that much more comfortable. He untied the horse from the tree, and with its reins in one hand and an opened bottle of beer in the other he started off once more.

The walking took longer than he had expected, now, of course, since he had become quite unsteady on his feet. In fact, by the time he had turned his steps south on the Capstone Road, and was heading out into the country, the night had grown very dark indeed.

There were no streetlights here, so that Kit had only the stars and the bright full moon hanging in the sky to show him his way. In his present state of mind, Kit found this rather romantic, and he began to sing softly to himself and the horse as they both plodded on through the night.

Suddenly a quiet voice interrupted Kit's rendition of 'The Lady in Red'. There, before him in the lane, stood a mysterious figure, a shadow among night shadows. Kit could make out no features of a face, but only the outlines of a broad-brimmed hat, a long cloak that swathed and concealed the stranger's whole body, and in his hand a great staff as high as a man is tall.

"*Well met, Kit Callot*", said the stranger.

It did strike Kit as odd that the stranger already knew his name, but for the first time in his life he knew instinctively that it was in his own best interests to be polite, so he returned the greeting.

"*Gd'evening*", he said.

"*Where might you be going at this time of the night, with such a fine horse?*" asked the stranger.

"*Taking it to the bloke who's bought it off me*", said Kit, "*It's not stolen or nothing*", he added defensively.

"*It must be hard to be working when a man should be settled in the tavern and drinking*", said the stranger,

"Perhaps I might save you much trouble by buying the horse from you myself".

And at that, he mentioned a sum of money so huge that Kit's jaw dropped and his eyes almost popped from his head with disbelief.

"You can have the horse, alright", said Kit, and the two of them shook hands on the bargain.

Said the stranger, *"Come with me, Kit Callot, and you shall have your just reward"*.

Kit, leading the horse, followed along a narrow side lane and up a steady slope, until the two of them came out onto a moonlit hillside. For the first time, Kit glimpsed the stranger's proud face; an aquiline nose, a long grey beard, and dark eyes that seemed to glimmer with their own inner light. The stranger strode over to a huge stone that lay upon the turf, and with the end of his staff he struck it three mighty blows. Before Kit's astonished gaze, a wide doorway swung slowly open in the earth and stone of the hillside itself.

Through that door and down a passageway Kit was led, deep into the heart of the hill. At last they came to a massive circular chamber, roofed with a dome. All around the chamber were stalls in which horses stirred and whinnied softly.

By every stall there was a couch, on each of which a knight reclined, sound asleep, already in full armour and with sword, lance and shield laid within easy reach. At the very centre of the hall was a round table.

The stranger took the reins of the horse from Kit's hand. He gestured casually to where, near to the table, caskets brimmed over-full with gold and jewels, spilling untold treasures heedlessly onto the floor of the chamber.

"Take what you are owed", he said, *"No more than that, and go back the way that you came to this place, and you will come to no harm"*. With that, he turned into a further passageway and, taking the horse with him, he simply seemed to vanish into thin air.

Several minutes passed by, dragging their feet, as Kit Callot stood stock still while his reeling mind tried to take in the situation. Then, barely breathing, he was among the caskets, stuffing priceless treasures, coins and glittering gems into every pocket with no regard to the stranger's advice. This took him some time, with many a pause for a sidelong look at the sleeping knights.

When he was certain that he could carry no more, Kit stood up, but now he had begun to grow curious. He went over to the round table itself and, for the first time, he saw that upon it there lay a magnificent sword, resplendent in a jewelled scabbard, and a great horn with a golden mouthpiece. All around the table an inscription glowed eerily.

"Awaken the sleepers, if you dare, to lead them forth on the day of need", Kit read, slowly.

Now some new and unfamiliar emotions began to stir in Kit's heart. He imagined himself leading the awakened knights out from the hill, his head swam with visions of riding at the head of his own army towards glory and...who knew what might be possible?

"King Kit Callot", he murmured aloud, trying the title out for size.

Yet he worried that if the knights should awake to see him brandishing a sword, they might regard him as an enemy and not wait to ask before treating him as such. So he left the sword where it was. Instead he lifted the horn in his two hands, placed the mouthpiece to his lips, took a deep breath, and blew with all his might.

The horn bellowed, and the deep note resounded around the chamber, down passageways into the furthest hidden corners of that ancient and mysterious place. Even before the last echoes of the horn had died away, Kit could hear an answering roar that seemed to swell from the very belly of the hill. The roaring grew steadily louder and louder, the great chamber and everything in it began to shudder until the entire hill, to Kit, felt as though it was trembling like a blancmange.

He was looking for something to hold onto for support when a wild and terrible blast of wind swept into the chamber. Kit was lifted bodily, off his feet, as the wind hammered into him and hurled him backwards; down the passageway and out through the portal onto the hillside. Kit lay flat on the ground where he fell, frozen with stark terror.

"*Woe to the coward, that he was ever born, that he should blow the horn before he drew the sword*", boomed a powerful voice. The door in the hill slammed shut with a force that shook the stars in the heavens, and Kit Callot slipped into a blessed unconsciousness.

When he came to, dawn was creeping across the land. He searched his pockets and found them to be empty, not a jewel or a single coin did he still have. He crawled around on the grass for a long time, but he had no luck, and eventually gave up the search. There was no trace of the portal on the hillside, nor was there any sign of the horse or of the stranger. Kit could only stumble home and tell his tale to the rest of his family.

I don't think any of them believed a single word, except perhaps the part about stopping off at the pub. By all accounts Kit's father, a harder case than Kit himself, gave the lad a vicious beating for his stupidity.

Ever since then, Kit Callot has been a changed man. He is quiet and restrained. His health seems broken too, his old strength seeping away from him, and he drinks far too much. You might meet him in a pub in Chatham, or in Luton village, and he will tell you this story and swear that it is true. Some people have said that he spends hours wandering the countryside around the Capstone Road, looking for something.

****

The legend of the sleepers beneath the hill may well be a familiar one. The faith that King Arthur and his company of warriors lie still beneath the land of Albion runs deep within the popular psyche. While this current of folk belief might have historical roots in the psychology of the Celtic population, longing for the rebirth of old glories and guarding against the possibility of further invasions, I feel that it has other, deeper, origins. That the tale of the sleppers in fact, represents an acknowledgement and awareness of the great forces that lie dormant below the surface of the Land.

Like most of the stories retold here, that of the sleepers is recurrent, the many variants all following the pathways of common themes, in spite of differences in detail and even tone. The differing versions are all distinguished by their localised nature. Arthur and his men have been said to sleep under, among other places, Alderley Edge in Derbyshire, or Craig y Dinas in Wales and - if the work of Dion Fortune is to be believed - in mysterious caverns beneath Glastonbury Tor in Somerset[2]. Time and time again the old belief, the ancient promise of the Once and Future King, bubbles up from the hills of Britain like spring water, to flow through the hopes and aspirations of ordinary folk.

This is one source of my own version of the legend, as written here. I make no pretence having told a traditional form of the story. Rather than merely recount an old version of the legend of the Sleepers Under the Hill - and, as I have mentioned, there are a number of them - I have fallen back, instead, upon a time-honoured technique of the storyteller's art. That is, while retaining the themes and the sense of the essential story, I have rewoven it to suit my own environment. Hence the transportation of the sleepers to the Twentieth Century and the Medway Valley. I should emphasise, at this point, the magical nature of the door into the hillside, and of the cavern beyond, and that no rewards await anybody who might try to dig into hills in a certain Country Park! The sleepers may wait, in truth, within the Land; but the doorway by which they may be found is accessible only through the consciousness of the seeker, and not in the Outer World.

Wherever the different versions of this legend may reappear, and in whatever guise, they contain a strong commonality of references. The waiting sleepers themselves; the halls beneath a hill; the ubiquitous Wise Man who stands guard over them; the avaricious fool who finds them, and his subsequent undoing. These elements form a recognisable refrain, the necessary core of the story.

It is the repetition of the cavern as a central motif which gives us a key to unlock the importance of the legend. Rather than moving through the Land, more or less freely and independently empowered, as do most characters of folk tale, these dormant warriors are cradled in a womb or alembic deep within the fertile earth; and they are unable to act without the agency of the proper seeker to stir them into life and awareness.

As for the mysterious Wise Man; it is one of the curiousities of this legend that it does not necessarily state in bald terms that the sleepers under the hill are Arthur and his companions. Instead, we are usually left to draw this as an inference from the narrative, but somehow we always do recognise the true identity of the sleepers. It is, similarly, usually implied that the Wise Man is none other than the great Merlin himself, whether an immortal individual mage, or the latest in a line of titular Merlins[3] who watch over the sleeping and vulnerable warriors until their moment of reawakening comes.

The fool appears, perhaps, as another key. We will return to look at his role further, in due course.

Why does this tale recur with such frequency and with so many familiar features? Clearly it resonates very strongly with the inhabitants of this island, for the promise of Arthur as Once and Future King still feeds, with some vigour, new shoots in art and literature. There is a trace, in this, of the ancient myth of the sacrificed and reborn God, tied to the turning wheel of the seasonal cycle; and, also, of Celtic aspirations for the recovery of their stolen homelands.

Yet, half-glimpsed behind the veil of the story, there seems to be something more. Perhaps this story, in its hidden caverns and its waiting warriors, embodies another reflection of the Utopian vision, the reawakening of a Golden Age.

The restoration of this lost Age, of a just and free Albion, is the promise embodied by the sleeping Arthur. When the sleepers awake, so the Land itself awakes also, and a new epoch is born from the stirring of the Underworld.

****

Exercise 11: The Hall Beneath the Hill

Settle yourself once more in a chair for meditation, and go through the usual preparations for visualisation work. Be comfortable, relax physically, and clear your mind of distractions from the everyday world. When you feel quite ready, close your eyes.

See before you, once more, a wooden doorway with no obvious handle or lock, arched at the top. The door itself is quite plain, except for the weathering and accumulated scars of great age. Wait patiently, until at last you hear a sound, as of a key turning on the far side of the door, and the door swings open silently.

Rising from your chair, you step across the threshold. You find yourself standing upon an earthen track. It is night, and the only light falls from a bright full Moon set against the deep blue canvas of the night sky. A few stars twinkle like sequins, and occasional clouds drift lazily over distant landscapes.

You look around yourself. Hedges rise high on either side of the track upon which you stand. You begin to walk. The track slopes gently downwards, and through the hedges you catch glimpses of open, ploughed fields. The night is strangely silent, and the Moon itself seems to be watching you in quiet expectation.

Now the lane is curving gently to the left, still leading down. Cloud slides across the face of the Moon, like a veil of smoke, and you suddenly find yourself in complete darkness. You pause, standing still awhile until your eyes are able to adjust to the lack of light. Gradually you begin to make out dim shapes again - the hedges to either side of you, the lane trailing ahead of your feet. Yet you cannot see far. You begin to walk forward once more, but more slowly and cautiously now.

You follow the sloping path downwards until, before you in the darkness, you hear the burbling sounds of a stream. You are aware that the water must be close by, and you pause in your walking while your eyes try to penetrate the night and find the stream.

As you search, you realise that just a little ahead of you there is a dark patch of shadow that seems to have the approximate shape of a human figure. The hairs prickle on the back of your neck as the sensation awakens that you are being watched intently. As you watch, with growing wariness, the still figure speaks in a male voice full of authority, and your heart leaps and begins to beat faster.

The dark man greets you and bids you not to be afraid. He tells you that he has come as a guide, and will lead you if you are willing to follow. You respond that you are prepared to go with him.

As you finish speaking, the clouds roll away from the face of the Moon, and the night is lit once more by its radiance. At last you can see properly the stranger who is your guide. He is a tall man, wearing a long black cloak, and a broad brimmed hat which seems to hide his face in shadow, although you are aware that his eyes seem to glitter with a hard inner light of their own. Behind him, at the foot of the slope, runs the swift stream that you could hear.

Your guide leads you to the bank of the stream and, by way of three stepping stones, across it to the far side. From here the path leads upward. You realise, as you follow behind the stranger, trying to keep up with his long stride, that you are climbing the side of a high hill, which is crowned with woodland. Soon the path enters these woods, the moonlight filtering between the trees to light your way.

You come to a clearing, the path opening up suddenly into it, and your guide stops abruptly. At the heart of the clearing you can see a great stone set into the slight rise of the ground. The stranger tells you to wait, and he walks forward to the stone. As if from nowhere, a long staff appears in his right hand. The tall man raises this aloft, and with a call he strikes a single blow with the staff upon the stone.

There is a deep, resonant booming which wells up from the depths of the hill until it seems to fill the entire clearing. A crack appears in the stone, running vertically, which grows to an ever widening fracture, until the stone is split entirely asunder.

Through the gap you can see the dark mouth of a tunnel that runs down into the belly of the hill, framed now by two rough pillars of stone. Your guide half-turns and beckons to you, and then he leads you between the two stone columns and into the passage. At his quick gesture, torches flare alight in brackets on either wall of the tunnel. Walls, floor and ceiling are all constructed of skilfully dressed stone. You are led downwards into the hill, the passage spiralling steadily to the left as you descend.

The stone passageway seems to turn three times counter-clockwise. And then opens out into a great chamber. Torches flare into light all around as your guide enters the hall, and you follow him into it. It is a vast natural cavern, circular and roofed with a high dome. At its centre stands a massive round table, constructed of heavy wood. On every side, set into the rock walls of the hall, there are many stables, and from each stable comes the sound of horses; whickerings, the shuffle and stamp of hooves, an occasional whinny.

It takes you a few moments to take all this in, aware as you are of its strangeness. Only then do you see that by the entrance of each stable there is a low couch, and upon each couch there lies the body of a sleeping knight, armed and armoured in readiness for battle.

You look for the stranger who has brought you here, to ask him the meaning of this mysterious place. But you find that he has gone, suddenly and silently, leaving you alone with the sleepers and with the questions that crowd so urgently in your mind.

Without his presence, you can only explore for yourself. Slowly, you begin to walk around the circumference of the huge round table. Take note of the type of armour being worn by the sleeping knights. Above each couch, there hangs a banner and a shield. Note, also, the designs upon these.

When you have walked right around the hall, you turn towards the table itself. You see that lying upon the table, within your reach, are a sword and a horn. The sword is a plain-looking broadsword, sheathed in a decorated scabbard. The horn tapers to a golden mouthpiece, and has a leather carrying strap. By them, an inscription is emblazoned across the table in letters of burning silver.

"Awaken the sleepers if you dare, to lead them forth on the day of need", the inscription reads.

You reach out and lift up the scabbarded sword. With your right hand you take a firm hold of the hilt, and then you draw the sword forth. Immediately the atmosphere in the hall changes. A shiver runs along the length of your spine, the sense of expectation is palpable.

At this point, if you feel unease, you might choose to resheathe the sword and replace it on the table; then return the way you have come, to the material world. You may be able to proceed further with this visualisation another time.

If you wish to carry on, you lay aside the scabbard and with your left hand take up the horn. You lift the mouthpiece to your lips and, summoning up your breath as best you can, you blow one long single note.

The deep bellow of the horn reverberates around the hall for long seconds. Then you feel a stirring in the earth beneath your feet. In the distance, there is a low rumble, which begins to grow louder and louder. Around you, the cavern is shuddering, the walls and floor and ceiling seem to be shaken by uncontrollable spasms. You wonder if you are experiencing some form of earthquake, and lean heavily against the round table to prevent yourself from falling.

Now the roaring noise is so overpowering that you feel deafened. The banners on the walls begin to lift and flap. Suddenly a fierce wind sweeps into the chamber. Caught unprepared, you are thrown back onto the table by its terrific impact. Your eyes closed, you are for a space unaware of anything but darkness and the power of the hurricane as it passes.

At last the force of the hurricane abates and dies down. You are able to open your eyes once more and raise yourself up. Sword and horn are both still grasped tightly in your hands. But you are astounded to find that you are now alone. The sleeping knights have arisen and have gone from the hall, along with their horses, their banners and their shields. The sleepers have ridden out into the world. Looking around, you notice that the inscription no longer glows upon the surface of the wooden table. There is nothing left for you to do but to leave.

You are aware that neither the sword nor the horn belong to you, they do not belong in the possession of any one individual, and so you place them on the round table as you found them.

Then you walk back by the way you have come. The ascending passage turns to the right, three times clockwise, until you emerge once more into the clearing on the hill. As you step into the glade, there is a grinding sound and, looking back, you see that the stone has closed to seal up the passageway and the hall beyond.

Follow the path through the woods, down to the stream; cross by the stepping stones, then walk up along the path until you reach the doorway from which you began this journey.

At your approach, the door swings open. Through it, you can see your chair. Step through the open doorway and sit down. You see the door close behind you, and hear a click as with a key being turned on the other side. Gradually return to full consciousness of the everyday world. When you have opened your eyes, "ground" yourself with a hot drink and something light to eat.

****

It is always the Fool who must be the catalyst which eventually awakens the sleeping powers within the Land. In the story, of course, it is the wrong kind of fool who is encountered. In the visualisation it is the true Fool, as seeker, who comes to the Hall Beneath the Hill; becoming, in the acts of drawing the sword and blowing the horn, a bridge between the hidden forces within the Unconscious and waking consciousness.

Workings such as this rarely succeed through being carried out once. They are a form of pattern within consciousness, which needs to be followed repeatedly, like creating a picture with the same stencil again and again. In this way the energies generated by the working become imprinted, over time, on the Inner levels of the consciousness, and are thus gradually enabled to take effect.

The worker joins with a broad company of women and men who, by myriad but eventually complementary means, are seeking to regenerate the Land. It is worth emphasising that such is a dialectical process. To work on Inner levels alone, through visualisations and similar methods, is not sufficient. It is, at the same time, vital to develop the direct relationship with the Outer forms of the Land; both in Nature, linking with the woods, hills and valleys that constitute our physical landscape, and in humankind, by healing and empowering the wounded and the disempowered.

I have chosen to use the term "worker" here with care. Much has been made, in some recent esoteric literature, of the imagery of Kings and Queens. The same symbolism tends to occur repeatedly in the realms of traditional stories (and hence in this book) too, but it is important to understand that these are Inner manifestations of some aspects of the self, and that to imagine that these might also develop in some Outer form is to fall heavily into the trap of illusion and fantasy. Then the Fool becomes merely a fool. In practice the task of regenerating the Land is a democratic process, open to all, whether you are a magician of many years' experience or a beginner taking your first hesitant steps upon the path.

Telling the Future

Somewhere, hidden from mortal eyes, there is a home for those who have acknowledged their place within the Land. They are the people who see more clearly through the mists of the future and the past, the people who walk lightly upon the Earth. In that place the stories are built into the fabric of the houses, are woven when women sit at the spinning wheel, are sown when men work in the fields. There is a story in the steps of a dance, the heartbeat of a drum, the call of a voice. There is a road that will lead us there, that will take us home. But finding the beginning of the road - that, too, is a story, and one that only we can tell.

We have come a long way from Rory O'Donoghue, the unstoried man in whose company we set out upon the journey. On our travels, we have stopped awhile at the tables of the ancestors and feasted ourselves on their tales, which are the storage jars of their old wisdom. Perhaps some little of that wisdom has been digested.

At the least, we have come closer in alignment with the Land in which their bones lie and upon which we tread. Note the term "alignment". We have not merely come closer to the Land. That would suggest a surgical separation from our own consciousness at some point in the past, a disconnection which is simply not possible. We have, rather, been de-storied to a greater or lesser degree in our literate, materialist civilisation, forgetting how to navigate the Land-scape in words and images. Not that literacy, material reality or civilisation are morally "bad" in and of themselves, but maybe we have lost our sense of balance through too exclusive a focus on them.

Restore that balance. Take the stories from this book and tell them. Take the stories from other pages, or better still, as gifts from the tongues of storytellers, and tell them. More so, tell the stories from your own life, from your own family. Tell the stories that you learn as you walk through the Land, in the woods, or in the deep and secret places of the psyche.

Every story is a seed that may be planted in the minds of others. From the seed, in time a tree may grow. The tree bears fruit; fruit that may - who knows until it is eaten? - give knowledge, or healing, or deep sleep and then rebirth.

Should you find the road, and walk along it until at last you come home, you must bear with you a gift. A gift for those who have travelled before you, leaving the markers that have shown you the way. Only one gift will do.

Here is a riddle, to tell you what you must take with you:

What is greater than the Gods, that the rich do not have, but that the poor have plenty of, that the dead may eat, and that the living may take with them when they die?

Riddle me this riddle...take it, and the stories you have heard, with my blessing.

Appendix

In this appendix I am giving the outline for a very simple, yet effective, means to both 'form' and 'close down' a ritual circle. The same comments made in reference to the rituals suggested in my chapter on *The Earth Will Have Its Own* also apply here.

Forming the Circle

Lay out a rope or cord to form a circle. Enter, and take up a small bowl of salted water and preferably a sprinkler (which can be made with a bunch of small twigs tied together at one end).

Say *"With this salted water, I bless this Circle, in the names of the Lord and Lady"*.

Moving clockwise around the Circle, sprinkle the salted water on the boundary. Once this has been completed, face North, raise both arms high in salute, and say:

"Lord and Lady, I request your presence to witness and bless this magical Circle, for I would make a place of worship in honour of you. I ask that you may guard me and guide me within this Circle, and that you may join with me in my rites".

Pause briefly to feel the subtle change in atmosphere within your Circle.

Say, "*Blessed be, the Lord and Lady*".

Closing Down the Circle

Raise both arms in salute and say:

"*I thank you, Lord and Lady, for your presence within this Circle. I take my leave of you now, in the spirit in which I have come before you; in the spirit of love, of peace and of trust. Blessed be, the Lord and Lady*".

This procedure is, as I say, very simple. With experience, it may be elaborated to become a powerful element of ritual. However, it is worth remembering that, in such work, inner intention is more important than outer display, and the simplest rituals are often the most effective.

Notes

The Place of Storytelling
1. A story first told to me by poet and storyteller Bill Lewis.

2, P. L. Travers, *About the Sleeping Beauty* (Collins 1977)

3. I first came across this story in *Folk Tales of the British Isles*, edited by Michael Foss (Macmillan 1977). I have heard other versions since - not surprisingly, this is a popular story theme with storytellers - in one version the role of the mysterious old man is taken by Pan.

4. And the moral is that one should always have a story to tell or a song to sing.

5. I first heard this story from the Irish-American storyteller Pat Ryan.

6. See Gareth Knight, *The Secret Tradition in Arthurian Legend* (Aquarian Press 1983), p. 198-200, for an esoteric view which explains this process in terms of polarity.

7. See, especially, Norma J. Livo and Sandra A. Rietz, *Storytelling: Process and Practice* (Libraries Unlimited 1986).

8. All this, of course, owes much to C. G. Jung and to Jungian psychology.

9. Engels, 'The Part Played by Labour in the Transition from Ape to Man", in *Marx Engels Collected Works*, vol 25 (London 1987). p 46.

The Mother of the Forest
Developed from a version that was originally collected by W. F. P. Burton in *The Magic Drum* (Methuen 1961).

1. See R. J. Stewart, *The Mystic Life of Merlin* (Arkana 1987).

2. A valuable exploration of animal symbolism from the pespective of native British tradition is Miranda Gray's *Beasts of Albion* (Aquarian Press 1994).

3. Janet and Colin Bord, *Enchanted Britain* (Thorsons 1995).

The Lake of the Seven Swans
A Fenland story, heard from Pat Ryan. Pat has recorded his version on a cassette, *Fill the House*, in collaboration with muscian Terry Mann.

1. Starhawk, *The Spiral Dance* (Harper & Row 1979).

2. A concept, apparently from psychosynthesis, that I learned early in my training as a counsellor.

3. For further guidance on visualisation and related meditative states, there are a number of valuable sources. These include Dolores Ashcroft-Nowicki, *The Shining Paths* (Aquarian Press 1983); Pete Jennings, *Pathworking* (Capall Bann 1995); Caitlin and John Matthews, *The Western Way* (Arkana 1985); Steve Hounsome, *Practical Meditation* (Capall Bann 1996).

The Lazy Man and the Water-Spirit
Another tale found in W. F. P. Burton's *The Magic Drum*.

1. "Crystal capitalism", as Bill Lewis recently described it.

The Harp on the Water
My source for this story was Gwyn Jones, *Welsh Legends and Folk Tales* (OUP 1955).

1. The finest book on Shelley, in my opinion, is Paul Foot's *Red Shelley* (Bookmarks 1984). There is an excellent analysis of *Prometheus Unbound* on p. 191-202.

2. At the time of writing, the British government might be regarded as an example of this attitude closer to home.

3. I am thinking, here, of the famous comment made by La Place. For a good antidote, from a scientific standpoint, it is worth reading

The Dancing Wu Li Masters by Gary Zhukav, and *The Tao of Physics* by Fritjof Capra.

The Discontented Grass Plant
Developed from a version in *The Penguin Book of World Folk Tales*, edited by Milton Rugoff (Penguin 1977).

1. I am using this term in a sense derived from Fritz Perl's Gestalt Therapy; to mean the whole cycle of the Land.

2. Miyamoto Musashi, *A Book of Five Rings*, translated by Victor Harris (Allison and Busby 1974).

3. Musashi, op. cit. See for example, p.44.

4, Which has many implications.

Who Owns the Land?
First heard in a version told by Taffy Thomas.

1. Many of the Nasrudin stories have been collected by Idries Shah, and can be found in three volumes: *The Pleasantries of the Incredible Mulla Nasrudin*, *The Subtleties of the Inimitable Mulla Nasrudin*, and *The Exploits of the Incomparable Mulla Nasrudin*.

2. A good version may be found in Carolyn McVicker Edwards, *The Storytellers' Goddess* (Harper Collins 1991).

3. Theodore Roszak, *Voice of the Earth* (Bantam 1993); Aida Gersie, *Earthtales* (Green Print 1992).

4. For those who wish to turn onto this particular pathway, men and women, I would recommend Marian Green, *A Witch Alone* (Aquarian Press 1991), as a starting point.

The Green Ladies of One Tree Hill
This story was originally drawn from Folk TAles of the British Isles, edited by Michael Foss (Macmillan 1977).

1. Tree Dressing Day pamphlet, Common Ground.

2. John Matthews, *Taliesin* (Aquarian Press 1991), p. 229-236.

3. 'The King and the Oak', in Alida Gersle, op. cit.

The Earth Will Have Its Own
From *The Penguin Book of World Folk Tales*, edited by Milton Rugoff (Penguin 1977).

1. As expressed in remakes of *Dracula*, in the novels of Anne Rice, in membership of the Vampire Society, etc.

2. Learned from various people within the Circle Dance network. But special mention must go to Stefan and Bethan Freedman, who teach a dance choreographed to this chant.

The Wildwood King
Adapted from the version collected by Italo Calvino, in *Italian Folktales* (Penguin 1982).

1. For more on the Horned God see, for example, Janet and Stewart Farrar, *The Witches' God* (Hale 1989); Nigel Jackson, *The Call of the Horned Piper* (Capall Bann 1995) and *Masks of Misrule*, (Capall Bann 1996).

2. The best known visual representation of this principle is the familiar Chinese "yin-yang" symbol.

3. I add this note for those readers who wonder at my focus, in this present book, largely upon the more masculine energies of the Land. I am now working on an accompanying exploration of the feminine aspects. Polarity has practical consequences.

Where the Sleepers Wait
My own variation on a traditional tale.

1. Janet and Colin Bord, op. cit.

2. Alan Richardson, *The Magical Life of Dion Fortune* (Aquarian Press 1991).

3. This latter concept of the Merlin may explain the appearance of Thomas the Rhymer in a Scottish version of the story. See Janet and Colin Bord, op. cit.

FREE DETAILED CATALOGUE

A detailed illustrated catalogue is available on request, SAE or International Postal Coupon appreciated. Titles are available direct from Capall Bann, post free in the UK (cheque or PO with order) or from good bookshops and specialist outlets. Titles currently available include:

Animals, Mind Body Spirit & Folklore
Angels and Goddesses - Celtic Christianity & Paganism by Michael Howard
Arthur - The Legend Unveiled by C Johnson & E Lung
Auguries and Omens - The Magical Lore of Birds by Yvonne Aburrow
Book of the Veil The by Peter Paddon
Caer Sidhe - Celtic Astrology and Astronomy by Michael Bayley
Call of the Horned Piper by Nigel Jackson
Cats' Company by Ann Walker
Celtic Lore & Druidic Ritual by Rhiannon Ryall
Compleat Vampyre - The Vampyre Shaman: Werewolves & Witchery by Nigel Jackson
Crystal Clear - A Guide to Quartz Crystal by Jennifer Dent
Earth Dance - A Year of Pagan Rituals by Jan Brodie
Earth Harmony - Places of Power, Holiness and Healing by Nigel Pennick
Earth Magic by Margaret McArthur
Enchanted Forest - The Magical Lore of Trees by Yvonne Aburrow
Familiars - Animal Powers of Britain by Anna Franklin
Healing Homes by Jennifer Dent
Herbcraft - Shamanic & Ritual Use of Herbs by Susan Lavender & Anna Franklin
In Search of Herne the Hunter by Eric Fitch
Inner Space Workbook - Developing Counselling & Magical Skills Through the Tarot
Kecks, Keddles & Kesh by Michael Bayley
Living Tarot by Ann Walker
Magical Incenses and Perfumes by Jan Brodie
Magical Lore of Cats by Marion Davies
Magical Lore of Herbs by Marion Davies
Masks of Misrule - The Horned God & His Cult in Europe by Nigel Jackson
Mysteries of the Runes by Michael Howard
Oracle of Geomancy by Nigel Pennick
Patchwork of Magic by Julia Day
Pathworking - A Practical Book of Guided Meditations by Pete Jennings
Pickingill Papers - The Origins of Gardnerian Wicca by Michael Howard
Psychic Animals by Dennis Bardens
Psychic Self Defence - Real Solutions by Jan Brodie
Runic Astrology by Nigel Pennick
Sacred Animals by Gordon MacLellan
Sacred Grove - The Mysteries of the Forest by Yvonne Aburrow
Sacred Geometry by Nigel Pennick
Sacred Lore of Horses The by Marion Davies
Sacred Ring - Pagan Origins British Folk Festivals & Customs by Michael Howard
Seasonal Magic - Diary of a Village Witch by Paddy Slade
Secret Places of the Goddess by Philip Heselton
Talking to the Earth by Gordon Maclellan
Taming the Wolf - Full Moon Meditations by Steve Hounsome
The Goddess Year by Nigel Pennick & Helen Field
West Country Wicca by Rhiannon Ryall
Witches of Oz The by Matthew & Julia Phillips

Capall Bann is owned and run by people actively involved in many of the areas in which we publish. Our list is expanding rapidly so do contact us for details on the latest releases.

Capall Bann Publishing, Freshfields, Chieveley, Berks, RG20 8TF Tel 01635 46455